The Business of Android Apps Development

Making and Marketing Apps That Succeed

Mark Rollins

Apress®

The Business of Android Apps Development: Making and Marketing Apps That Succeed

ISBN-13 (pbk): 978-1-4302-3942-0

ISBN-13 (electronic): 978-1-4302-3943-7

President and Publisher: Paul Manning
Lead Editor: Tom Welsh
Technical Reviewer: Bradley D. Brown
Editorial Board: Steve Anglin, Mark Beckner, Ewan Buckingham, Gary Cornell, Morgan Engel, Jonathan Gennick, Jonathan Hassell, Robert Hutchinson, Michelle Lowman, James Markham, Matthew Moodie, Jeff Olson, Jeffrey Pepper, Douglas Pundick, Ben Renow-Clarke, Dominic Shakeshaft, Gwenan Spearing, Matt Wade, Tom Welsh
Coordinating Editor: Corbin Collins
Copy Editor: Damon Larson
Compositor: Bytheway Publishing Services
Indexer: SPI Global
Artist: SPI Global
Cover Designer: Anna Ishchenko

Distributed to the book trade worldwide by Springer Science+Business Media, LLC., 233 Spring Street, 6th Floor, New York, NY 10013. Phone 1-800-SPRINGER, fax (201) 348-4505, e-mail orders-ny@springer-sbm.com, or visit www.springeronline.com.

For information on translations, please e-mail rights@apress.com, or visit www.apress.com.

Apress and friends of ED books may be purchased in bulk for academic, corporate, or promotional use. eBook versions and licenses are also available for most titles. For more information, reference our Special Bulk Sales–eBook Licensing web page at www.apress.com/bulk-sales.

The source code for this book is available to readers at www.apress.com.

Contents at a Glance

Contents

About the Author

Mark Rollins was born in Seattle in 1971, and graduated Washington State University in 1994 with a degree in English. After college, he began to write skits for college-age groups. After four years working for Walmart, and another five years working for Schweitzer Engineering Laboratories (SEL), he decided to pursue a full-time career in writing. Since then he has written for many tech and gadget blogs, including screenhead.com, image-acquire.com, cybertheater.com, mobilewhack.com, carbuyersnotebook.com, gearlive.com, zmogo.com, gadgetell.com, gadgets-weblog.com, and coolest-gadgets.com. He has also written for video game blogs such as gamertell.com and digitalbattle.com. He recently began writing for the Android blog androidedge.com. Mark currently resides in Pullman, Washington with his wife and three children.

About the Technical Reviewer

■ **Bradley D. Brown** is a Senior Managing Partner and Chief Technology Officer of Breosla LLC, a business acceleration company he co-founded with Kevin Fallon. Breosla (www.breosla.com) leverages private equity and business process design, strategy, and execution for superior value creation. Breosla invests in software-related business model innovation opportunities where it can change or improve how a business creates, delivers, and retains value. An investing and operating company, it works primarily on cloud/SaaS, collaboration, enterprise, security, and mobile opportunities. Within Breosla are three areas of competency: Breosla Consulting that engages with established and expansion stage companies to accelerate business performance; Breosla Advisors, a licensed investment banking practice that helps portfolio companies with investment strategy and merger/acquisition (M&A) activity; and Breosla Partners, recently formed to launch and manage Breosla Partners I LP, a private equity fund.

Prior to Breosla, Brad founded and is a board advisor of TUSC, an international Oracle software consultancy. Vast experience earned Brad roles as acting CTO and board member for many companies over 23+ years at TUSC. Brad has published many applications in the Android markets. He has been a startup CTO and actively involved in IT since the early 1980s. He worked for Pioneer, Midwest Stock Exchange, and Oracle. Brad has written five technical books on Web Development in the Oracle world. He is the author of several best-selling Oracle Press books, and Oracle awarded him the honorary title of Oracle ACE Director. Brad taught "New Venture Creation" at the University of Denver's Daniels College of Business. In 2009, his alma mater, Illinois State University put Brad into their first Hall of Fame for Applied Science and Technology. Brad holds a BS in Applied Computer Science from Illinois State University.

Brad may be reached at brad.brown@breosla.com and followed on bradleydbrown.blogspot.com.

Acknowledgments

I would like to give special acknowledgement to the following people:

Brian Dorgan, who gave me terrific advice for programming on Android. I wouldn't have been able to write half the things in this book if not for his advice.

Wallace Jackson, who wrote the Apress book *Android Apps for Absolute Beginners* and inspired me to write Android applications of my own.

Steve Anglin, whom I first met at CES 2011 and who helped grant me the opportunity to write for Apress.

Corbin Collins and his editorial team, as their good advice helped me to create this work. It has been a busy few months, but I am proud to say it is complete.

Geoff Webb, who helped me while I took my first programming course at Washington State University.

Kristina Rollins, my beautiful wife and the mother of my three wonderful children.

Al Carlton, who gave me a terrific opportunity for writing for coolest-gadgets.com for many years.

Preface

It's probably easier to explain what this book isn't, rather than go into detail about what it is. If you are looking for a book that will teach you exactly how to write Android programs, this is not that book.

This is not to say that I won't be discussing how to construct an Android app, but I just won't go into great detail. My purpose is to make certain that you, the successful Android developer, are pointed in the right direction. If help in programming Android apps is the type of help you need, then you might want to check out some other books from Apress, such as the following:

- *Android Apps for Absolute Beginners*, by Wallace Jackson (Apress 2011)

- *Beginning Android 3*, by Mark Murphy (Apress 2011)

- *Pro Android 3*, by Satya Komatineni, Sayed Hashimi, and Dave MacLean (Apress 2011)

- *Pro Android Web Apps*, by Damon Oehlman and Sébastien Blanc (Apress 2011)

- *Android Essentials*, by Chris Haseman (Apress, 2008)

- *Learn Java for Android Development*, by Jeff Friesen (Apress 2010) (note that this book is only about the subset of Java you need to program on Android; it says nothing about Android itself)

It is of course essential that the Android developer learn as much about programming as possible to pursue a career in original application development. However, what is almost as important is what to do once that incredible mobile program has been created. That's where this book comes in. Proper marketing, promotion, and advertising could be the difference between major and minor profits for your application. If you are in the business to make money from your Android mobile software, then the information contained within these pages is going to make a significant difference.

Much of the focus of this book is geared toward the marketing of an Android application, but I touch on specific aspects of programming and app creation.

Chapters 1 through 3 discuss how to conceive the idea of a well-marketed application, and what tools you will need to build this application. Chapters 4 through 9 are all about what marketing steps you need to take as you are building the application, in anticipation for the launch date. Chapters 10 and 11 discuss what to do after the launch date and how to keep momentum going on your application so it will continue to make you money for years to come. Chapter 12 talks about how to program with Android and the Eclipse IDE. The following lists details what's covered in each chapter.

- *Chapter 1:* This chapter introduces Android in general and talks about its origins and development as a platform.

- *Chapter 2:* As you well know, the Android Market is flooded with applications, so you need to find out what sets yours apart. Chapter 2 discusses what you can do to produce a work that will be in demand, how to analyze the competition, where to find your target audience, and even how to name your application. Chapter 2 also discusses what you need to do to protect the intellectual property of your application.

- *Chapter 3:* Chapter 3 discusses how to narrow your target audience by introducing culture into everything your application does. This includes making the user interface, the icon, the logo, and the web site follow a specific theme.

- *Chapter 4:* Once you have decided on a look and theme for your application, it's time to create a marketing plan for when it is released. You should determine your marketing strategy based on what media outlets you want to report on your Android application. This includes blogs, printed media, social networks, and other methods of spreading the word about your application, including word-of-mouth (the best *and* worst marketing method).

- *Chapter 5:* As a developer, you might want to create several applications. Chapter 5 shows how you can use one app to promote other apps you have developed. It also shows how to promote applications on social networks like Twitter and Facebook, as well as how to prompt users to review your applications, which will lead to more downloads.

- *Chapter 6:* Just because you are giving away an app for free on the Android Market doesn't mean that you can't get something out of it. This chapter will discuss creating a lite version of your app along with a paid version. Chapter 6 also discusses ad revenue, as well as affiliate programs to maximize profits.

- *Chapter 7:* The initial price of your app isn't the only way to make money from an application; there are several other methods, including in-app billing. This is when the application sets up a store for selling virtual goods, such as rewards within a game. This chapter shows how to put it in your program.

- *Chapter 8:* At this point, you should be just about ready to publish the application to the Android Market. In order to avoid work after your prerelease date, you should prepare a press release and get the word out on social networks and your application's website.

- *Chapter 9:* The Android Market is a lot simpler to get into than Apple's App Store, because there is no approval process. However, there *are* a lot of hoops to jump through before you can get your application on the Android Market. This chapter discusses the process, including digital signing, keystores, and creating an Android Market account.

- *Chapter 10:* Once your application is out on the market, it is time to let everyone know. Chapter 10 shows the easiest way to send out multiple e-mails, as well as how to inform potential users via social networks and other methods of promotion. The more people that know about your application, the better chance it has of selling.

- *Chapter 11*: Now that the app is out there, you can take other steps to ensure its success. Chapter 11 shows you steps that need to be taken in order to ensure that profits increase and the application lives on.

- *Chapter 12*: This chapter is for those who are using Eclipse IDE for the first time, and teaches basic Java SE programming commands. Also included is a sample application so you can see these tools in action.

The Android Application Business

The mobile application business model is essentially the new get-rich-quick scheme. There are many who put out their app on smartphone platforms, and begin to start receiving profits from users, advertisers, and shops within their applications. There is, of course, a lot of work involved before the developer can simply sit back and watch the money roll in.

This was certainly the case for iOS during the big app boom of the iPhone launch of 2007, and there is no question that the Android Market has been influenced by Apple's App Store. I will talk about their specific similarities and differences later, but for now, I want to discuss the Android Market in general.

The State of the Android Market

Android, with its services on phones and tablets, is a pretty good market to be in right now. In May 2011, Google announced that there had been 3 billion applications downloaded from the Android Market. Just a few months prior to that, there were approximately 30,000 free and paid applications available to Android users. This number grew to 30,000 from 16,000 in exactly three months. By the time that this book is published, I am sure that the Android Market will have over 100,000 applications, and I wouldn't be surprised if that growth is even faster than anticipated.

Dividing the March figure of 3 billion applications downloaded by the figure of 30,000 available applications, it means that every Android application, on average, has had 100,000 downloads.

Sure, that last number looks pretty good, but it is just a statistic. There is no guarantee that your brand-new Android application will have that number. Also keep in mind that a lot of these applications are free, which is helpful in achieving the greater-than-average number of downloads. I will detail in this book later how to have a free application and still make profits, but you should know that there is a paid download for every 100 downloads, and some say that figure is as high as 1,000 to 1.

As an example, *Angry Birds*, by Rovio, is free for Android users, and it is a mobile game giant that has produced massive funds for the company. The mobile game had over 2 million Android downloads in the three days after its Android release, and 7 million Android downloads one month after that. These stats are over a year old, and Rovio, the game's developers, are still finding ways to make money on the Angry Birds franchise with spin-off applications, merchandise, and more.

You will soon discover that the massive amount of Android applications on the market can work against the developer, as the Android Market is flooded with applications of all types. This means that one application, as great as it might be, can get lost in the crowd and become very difficult to be noticed by its intended audience. If a developer markets their application so it gets a lot of publicity, Android users might pay to download one type of application, even though a similar version with more features is readily available for free.

Go to the Android Market on a web browser. You will see a slideshow that you can browse through on your Android's device touchscreen or your browser (see Figure 1-1). You will also see a list of featured apps. On the web version, you'll see the following lists of apps as well: Top Paid, Top Free, Top Grossing,

Top New Paid, and Top New Free. Yes, you can probably make more from your app if you are on these lists, as your app will be easier to find by random Android users. However, there are ways of making money from your app even if you are not on anyone's Featured list.

Figure 1-1. *A quick peek at the Android Market, from a web browser. Note the Featured section, the Top Paid list, and the slideshow of application ads.*

Before we can start talking about how to make money with Android, let's talk about some Android basics.

The Origins of Android

Android Inc. was a small startup company that developed its own open source operating system for mobile phones. It was bought by Google in August, 2005.

In November 2007, shortly after Apple introduced the iPhone, Google began working on its contribution to the mobile phone business. It announced the start of the Open Handset Alliance (OHA), which is a consortium of companies such as HTC, Motorola, Samsung, Sprint, T-Mobile, and other big names in the telecommunications industry. On the very same day, OHA unveiled the mobile operating system that we know today as Android.

Android got off to a slow start with the HTC Dream (also known as the T-Mobile G1) in October 2008. Since then, Android has been gaining popularity with the release of every new version. It is important that you know about them when you begin developing Android applications, as newer versions contain more features than their predecessors. In terms of programming, these versions have a definite numerical designation. I will discuss that when we get into downloading Android development tools like the Android SDK (Software Development Kit) and Eclipse.

For now, you should know that in addition to a specific number, Android versions also have an informal name, which is always named after some sweet treat. This is partly due to tradition and Google's sense of humor. This naming convention is also alphabetical, having begun with Cupcake, followed by Donut, Éclair, Froyo, Gingerbread, Honeycomb, and most recently Ice Cream Sandwich.

Here is a very basic summary of the features of the latest versions of Android:

- Version 1.5 (Cupcake):

    - Ability for videos to be recorded through camcorder

    - Bluetooth enabling

    - Widgets on home screen

    - Animated screen capabilities

    - Uploading of videos to YouTube and pictures to Picasa on the fly

- Version 1.6 (Donut):

    - Camcorder, camera, and integrated gallery

    - Voice search

    - Voice dial

    - Bookmark

    - History

    - Contacts search

    - WVGA screen resolution

    - Google turn-by-turn navigation

- Version 2.0/2.1 (Éclair):

    - HTML5 and Exchange Active Sync 2.5 support

    - Improved speed

    - Google Maps 3.1.2

    - MS Exchange Server integration

    - Flash for the camera

    - Bluetooth 2.1 integration

    - Option of virtual keyboard

- Version 2.2 (Froyo):

    - 320dpi screen with 720p

    - JIT compiler

    - Chrome with JS engine version 8

- Wi-Fi hotspot tethering
- Bluetooth contacts sharing
- Adobe Flash support for version 10.1
- Ability for apps to be installed on expandable memory, such as SD cards

- Version 2.3 (Gingerbread):
  - Improved gaming graphics and audio effects
  - SIP VoIP support
  - WXGA (extra-large screen size and resolution)
  - Near field communication
  - Copy/paste feature
  - Download manager for large downloads
  - Better control of applications
  - Support for multiple cameras

- Version 3.0 (Honeycomb):
  - The first tablet-only release
  - 3D desktop with newer widgets
  - Tabbed web browsing
  - Gtalk video chat
  - Hardware acceleration
  - Multicore processor
  - Multipane navigation

- Version X (Ice Cream Sandwich):
  - Streamlined user interface fit for both tablets and smartphones
  - Advanced app framework

You will discover that specific Android devices start out as one particular version of Android, and upgrades tend to come out slowly. It depends on the carriers, and often subscribers don't hear when the new updates come out. For example, I updated my Droid X from Froyo to Gingerbread, but Verizon didn't inform that an update was readily available. I only heard about the update because of my work in tech blogging, and someone else figured out how to give me the update. If you are curious about discovering whether you have the most current version on your Android device, click its Settings icon, select About Phone, and then select System Updates.

You will also discover that knowing about these versions of Android will be helpful when programming new applications. Later versions of Android devices are reverse (backward) compatible, which means that an Android 2.2 device will play an Android 1.6 program. However, Android apps designed for latter versions may not play on devices on former versions. For example, a version 1.6 Android device will not be able to use an app programmed for Android 2.2. In fact, if you have a device that runs 1.6 and do a search on the Android Market for an application designed for versions 2.2 or above, it will not even show up in the results.

By the way, a lot of low-priced Android phones still run very early versions of Android; for this reason, it might be wise to create a program that can run on Android 1.5 or 1.6 rather than only version 2.0 or above. Unless you have specific tablet-based application in mind, do not program with Android 3.0. Version 3.0 is optimized for tablets, not for smartphones. Right now, the Honeycomb market is limited to a few models, and until more models are made (which could be soon) it could take a while before a developer can make money off of it.

Android vs. iOS

When the iPhone was first unveiled, a new sort of business model was established for consumer electronics. While Steve Jobs and his friends at Apple were not the first to invent the touchscreen, they were able to create a new type of software enterprise that was personable and utilitarian. Apple's "there's an app for that" slogan has proven to users that the mobile software that they need should be readily available where and when they need it. It works for the smartest engineer and the dumbest consumer, and it has created a new type of software market.

As of this writing, Apple is a monster when it comes to apps. In fact, there is a little bit of a legal suit on who has the rights to the word *app*, and I'm guessing that it won't be settled by the time this has been published. Android may not currently have the high numbers that Apple has, but its market is ever-growing.

In February 2011, Google CEO Eric Schmidt stated that Android activations reached about 350,000 per day. At a recent I/O developer conference last May, it was revealed that there were 400,000 new activations per day, not to mention 450,000 developers and 215 carriers. That is about 100 million total activations overall as of May 2011. In comparison, Steve Jobs stated in March 2011, during his presentation of the iPad 2, that over 100 million iPhones have been activated. It would appear that Android's 100 million devices in May 2011 means that Android is catching up quickly. In short, the Android market is presently booming, and if any software has a chance to eclipse Apple's huge dominance over the app industry, it's Android.

When Steve Jobs announced the iPad 2, he ribbed that Honeycomb only had 100 applications while the iPad had hundreds of thousands. That figure was slightly biased, as Honeycomb had been around for only one month. Also, many Android smartphone applications work on Honeycomb.

As a developer, you should know how Android compares to iOS at least at some level. Apple iOS is a proprietary operating system, while Android is open source, which means it gives users the right to use, study, change, and improve design through ready availability of the source code. It uses the Linux kernel software for all of its versions. This is different from iOS, which works only on Mac products. This is one of the reasons why the Android operating system is so popular on smartphones and tablets, and will probably have a significant presence in televisions in the near future: it is not required to be tied to any particular device manufacturer.

Another way that Android differs from Apple is that Android has no approval process when it comes to apps. Once the user has signed up, uploading and publishing becomes a relatively simple process. (This is different for when you submit to Amazon's Android market, and we will discuss Amazon's approval process in later chapters.)

Also, you should know that Google reserves the right to yank your application off Android Market, even after you are already on it. A lot of applications are removed due to NSFW (not-suitable-for-work) content, but they can easily be yanked for other reasons as well.

Porting Difficulties

For those who want to turn their iOS app into a full-fledged Android application (or vice versa), I want to let you know the process and pitfalls.

If you haven't written an app for iOS, you might want to skip this section if you are thinking that you just want to market your application for the Android Market. However, I'm going under the assumption that you are trying to monetize as much as possible, so you might consider turning your Android application into an iOS application. I will cover how to do that by the end of this chapter.

Let's say you've written an iOS app that is out right now, or perhaps waiting in the app approval process. To turn it into an Android application, you will have to adapt your software so that an executable program can be created for a computing environment that is different from the one that it was originally designed for. This is known as porting.

Most of the iOS apps on the iTunes Store are written in Objective-C, while Android is specifically Java and XML. Although the logic of these programming languages is quite similar, as they are both linear, procedural, and use notions of object orientation (OO), they are very different with respect to OS support, GUI objects, and application life cycle. Sadly, Objective-C is not supported on Android.

As far as I can tell, there doesn't seem to be some magical program that will allow you to insert iPhone apps in and get Android applications out (unless you use development tools that have this in mind from the beginning). I will take a moment to talk about cross-platform development tools later, but let me discuss what you can do for both Android and iOS.

Your iOS coding cannot be reused for Android coding, but it does not mean that you have to rewrite all your Android code from scratch. For example, you can completely reuse the icons and images, as well as any SQLite database code.

Generally, it usually takes the same amount of effort to port an iOS app to Android as it does to create it. Hopefully it will take less time, but I can't guarantee that. It really depends on how big the application is, as well as the complexity of the code, reliance on GUI tools, and the ability of the developer.

By the way, there are people who make it their business to program apps, and that could lighten your workload. The same case exists for those who are into porting iOS apps to Android applications.

If you have written your iOS app in ANSI C or C++, such as in the many gaming engines that come out for such a purpose, then you are in luck. Android has the Native Development Kit (NDK), which allows for ANSI C or C++ code to be used with a Java layer for interface. If you go with the NDK, you will not have to use the Android SDK, which I will describe later.

Examples of Cross-Platform Development Tools

Chances are you want your application to be downloaded as much as possible, which means that you probably want it to be on many devices as possible. If you want to have your application on both iOS and Android, as well as other mobile platforms, you are going to have to do this from the beginning with certain cross-platform development kits.

Allow me to explain that I cannot testify to the success of such programs as these. I believe that the application market is headed in the direction where one developer's toolkit will work for all platforms, but, as explained before, we are not quite there yet. For the sake of the subject matter of this book, I only discuss how to use the Java JDK (Java Development Kit), the Android SDK, and the Eclipse IDE (integrated development environment) to construct Android applications. I will explain these programs later, but I wanted to discuss a few cross-platforms development kits, just so you know that there are alternatives.

Livecode

Livecode is the work of RunRev, a company that creates development tools. In the words of Ben Beaumont, product manager for RunRev, Livecode is "a multi-platform element environment that [has] now been moved to the mobile space." Livecode was originally made for Mac, Windows, and Linux, and it boasts "compile-free coding." Compile-free coding means that when you make a change to your program, you will see it as you are programming. This is different then the usual method of editing, compiling, running, and debugging.

Livecode also has a visual development environment, where the user can drag and drop the objects and images that will make up the final interface. The user can then attach scripts to these objects to really bring them to life, as well as lend them speed. Livecode uses a very high-level language, which allows the user to write in code that is very close to English. This allows you to write in this code easily, and the code will be easier to read. All this allows for the creation of live prototypes that actually run on the device, and promises to make it easy to work with clients, as you can more directly show them what you want, rather than showing them stagnant code.

Appcelerator

Titanium has created a free and open source application development platform that allows the user to create native mobile, tablet, and desktop application experiences. Their Appcelerator program allows the user to build applications full of features, as if they were written in Objective-C or Java. The end results are native apps that are customizable with a lot of features, all built with the web technology of JavaScript.

They allow developers to concentrate on building the application and provide a toolset for many platforms.

appMobi XDK

appMobi's mobile app development XDK is made for web developers. appMobi's claim is that if you can build an application for the web using HTML, CSS, and JavaScript, then you can build it as an application on the iPhone, the iPad, and Android smartphones and pads. According to their appMobi, developers can develop robust, 100 percent native API–compliant mobile applications in hours using preferred editors, and write once to deploy for all target platforms.

XDK includes an onscreen emulator with simple, approachable tool palettes to simulate user interaction with a testing device. It also allows you to send your application project over a local Wi-Fi connection or upload to the cloud to test it from anywhere. As a warning, you will need Java 6 and Google Chrome 6.0 to even begin running this program.

appMobi also offers a service known as MobiUs, which allows any app publisher to offer its app from anywhere on the Web, which could mean the end of frustrating and complicated processes of submission and approval to traditional app distributors (and also the end of developers needing to share their profits with these distributors). It is also cloud-based, which means it is possible to create iPhone apps on a Windows PC and Android applications on a Mac.

PhoneGap

According to its web site, PhoneGap allows users to build apps with web standards based on HTML 5. PhoneGap users can also access native APIs in order to create applications for multiple platforms, including iOS, Android, Windows, BlackBerry, webOS, and more. PhoneGap is currently in version 1.0.0.

Getting Started As an Android Developer

As I mentioned before, it is necessary to know a lot about programming in order to be an Android developer. Android programs are written in Java, a specific type known as the Dalvik virtual machine. The name *Dalvik* comes from the original writer, Dan Bornstein, who named it after a fishing village in Eyjafjörður, Iceland. It would be easy to write a whole book on the Dalvik virtual machine, and this has actually been done: *Beginning Java Google App Engine*, by Kyle Roche and Jeff Douglas (Apress, 2009). In addition to knowing Java, you are probably going to have to know some XML, as parts of the framework for Android use this markup language.

As mentioned before, this book is geared toward the marketing aspect of Android development. If programming isn't you're thing, there is no reason why you cannot hire someone to program your app and then do all the marketing yourself. For example, you can go to ODesk (https://www.odesk.com/) and hire a developer, as this web site is designed to outsource to all kinds of freelancers. However, I would advise you to download the basic toolkits for making Android apps so that you have a better chance of refining your app later.

There are three programs that you will need to get started:

- The Java JDK

- The Android SDK

- The Eclipse IDE

Beyond just getting these programs, you'll have to make sure that they are configured to work together as well.

The JDK

The JDK is a necessary part of your Android development package. It was made by Sun Microsystems, and later purchased by Oracle in 2009. The JDK is absolutely free, and here is what you need to do to get it:

1. Open an Internet browser and go to www.oracle.com/technetwork/java/javase/downloads/index.html.

2. You will see a lot of choices of what to pick, but you can simplify the process by clicking the JDK that is listed under the steaming Java logo download (on the left in Figure 1-2).

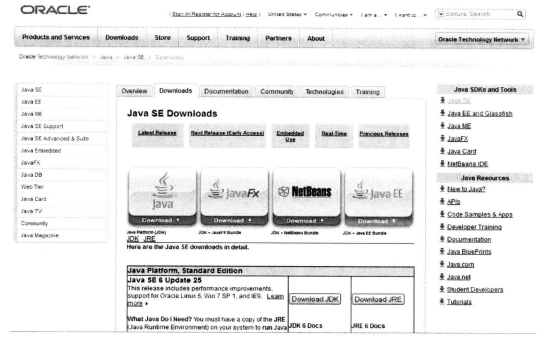

Figure 1-2. *Clicking the Download JDK button under Java SE 6 Update should work well for you to get the Java JDK.*

3. You will then be asked to accept the license agreement and select the proper product/file description for your operating system (see Figure 1-3). For most users, this will be Windows X86. Please note that I say "most," and you should check your computer for what operating system is best.

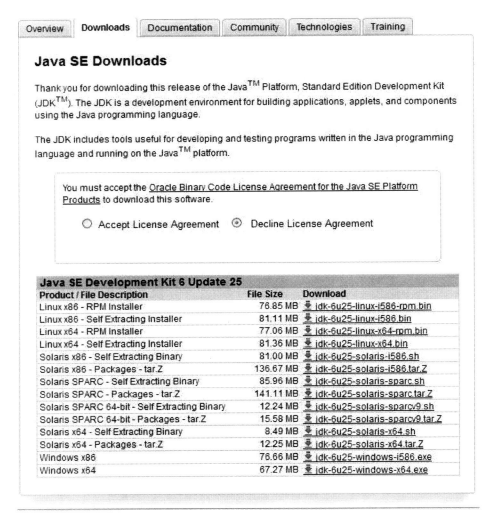

Figure 1-3. The license agreement for the Java JDK, as well as the product and file descriptions

4. Save the JDK program to whatever file you want.

5. Click the file to install the JDK.

The Android SDK

SDK contains many tools, such as libraries, a debugger, a handset emulator, documentation, sample code, and even tutorials. Here's how to download and install it:

1. You should be able to get the SDK here for Windows, Mac OS X, and Linux:
    http://developer.android.com/sdk/index.html.

2. Select the version you need (Windows, Mac OS X, or Linux 386) and download
    (see Figure 1-4).

Figure 1-4. *The Android Developer's web site, where developers can get Android SDK for free.*

3. If you haven't downloaded the Java JDK, the SDK download will not work. The
    JDK should automatically detect that program and start downloading the SDK.
    On some occasions, I have tried to download the SDK, and have received a
    message telling me that I don't have the JDK, even though I had just
    downloaded it. If this happens to you, click Back in the window, and then click
    Next. For some reason, this has been known to fix this problem.

4. Once it downloads the SDK, you can select a title for it on the Start Menu if you
    like.

5. Eventually, you will come to a screen that will allow you to choose what sort of
    packages to install (see Figure 1-5).

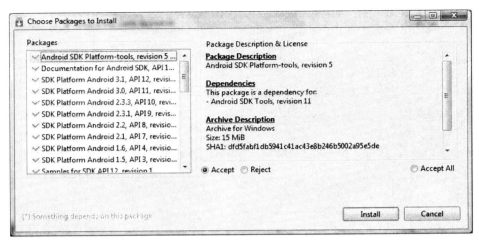

Figure 1-5. *The Android SDK user can choose what kinds of Android development programs to install.*

Note Depending on what version of Android you want to make apps for, choosing what packages to install could be very important. If you're doing programs for Honeycomb, then you might not feel a need to download Android 1.6. These programs take a long time to download, and if you decide that you want them later, then you can get them again, as they will be available. By the way, you have to click the ones that you don't want, and click Reject if you don't want them. My recommendation is to download everything from 1.6 to the newest version of Android, and you can skip version 3.0 unless you want to develop an application that is optimized for tablets.

Depending on how many packages you want, and the speed of your Internet connection, it might take a long time to download. You should eventually see a screen like the one in Figure 1-6, letting you know exactly what packages you did or didn't install. Clicking on the Installed packages on the column on the left shows the ones that you have downloaded, and clicking on the Available packages shows you what you did not (and still can) install.

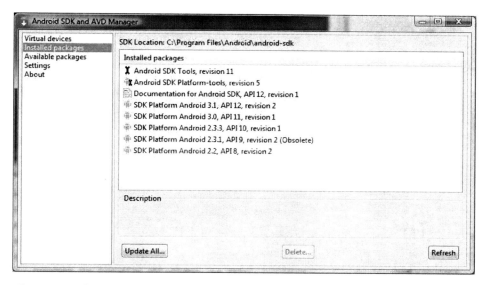

Figure 1-6. After the packages have been downloaded, you should see this confirmation screen.

The Eclipse IDE

The Eclipse IDE is where the development of your Android application happens. Here's how to get it up and running:

1. You should be able to find the correct version for downloads at the appropriately named URL: http://eclipse.org/downloads/ (see Figure 1-7). I recommend the Eclipse IDE for Java Developers.

Figure 1-7. The Eclipse IDE is also available to download for free.

2. When you have downloaded Eclipse, it will show up as a ZIP file. Open up the file.

3. Click the eclipse.exe file, and create a shortcut on your desktop if you like (see Figure 1-8).

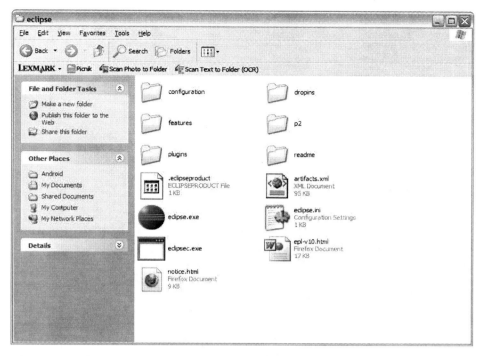

Figure 1-8. What you will see when you open up the folder for Eclipse after it downloads.

4. You'll see a window for Workspace Launcher, so you should set up a destination for your workspace if you haven't already. Since you are probably going to have multiple workspaces that you will want to create for your career as an Android application developer, you should come up with different names for every individual application (see Figure 1-9).

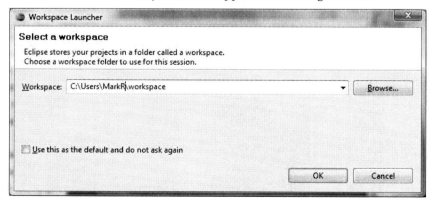

Figure 1-9. You'll want to create several workspaces for creating Android applications.

5. Eventually, you are going to come to the welcome screen. On that screen, notice the spotted area with icons that represents features. From left to right, you will see the icons for Overview, What's New, Samples, Tutorials, and Workbench (see Figure 1-10).

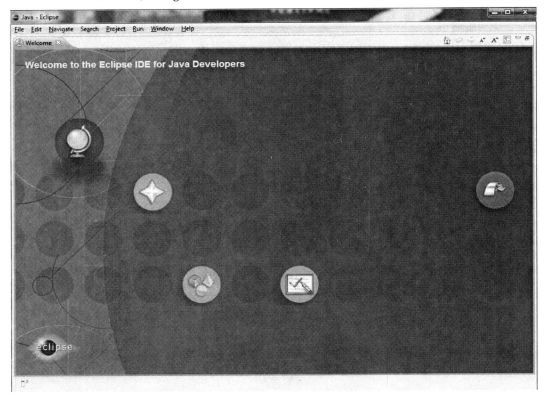

Figure 1-10. The Eclipse IDE welcome screen

6. Click the Workbench icon (the one with the curved arrow), and you should see a screen similar to the one in Figure 1-11. If you do not see this screen, then you have a different version of the Eclipse IDE than the one in Figure 1-11.

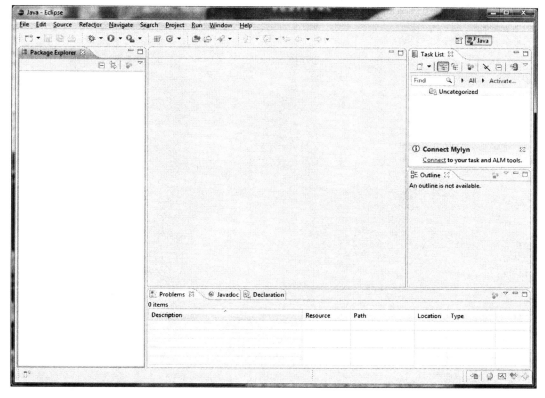

Figure 1-11. A typical workspace on Eclipse

7. Once you have Eclipse working, you should be able to get a plug-in known as
    Android Development Tools (ADT). It will help you create an integrated
    environment for building Android applications. Start by going to the Eclipse
    menu bar, where it says Help. Click there, and go to Install New Software.

8. You will see a window that looks like Figure 1-12. In this window, click the
    button marked Add.

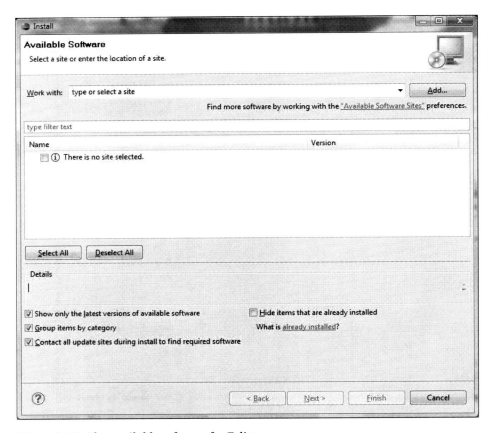

Figure 1-12. The available software for Eclipse

9. You will then see another window. You will need to type something in the Name field, or select it using the down arrow to the left of the "Add" button. If Eclipse allows you to select it, go ahead and pick https://dl-ssl.google.com/android/eclipse in the Location area, or you can type it manually (see Figure 1-13).

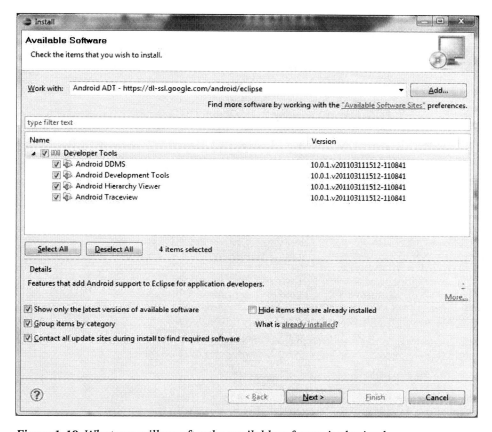

Figure 1-13. What you will see after the available software is obtained

10. You will then see a list of items under Developer Tools. Click the check box next to Developer Tools and select individual ones, and then click Next. You can then review the software licenses and click Finish.

11. In the next window, you'll be prompted to restart your computer. Click Restart Now.

12. Go ahead and open up Eclipse when your computer is powered up. On the menu bar, click Windows and choose Preferences. Select the button marked Android. Make certain to select the same workspace that you had before.

13. You can then set the SDK location to `C:\android\android-sdk-windows`.

How to Use Your Own Android Device As an Emulator on Eclipse

As you develop applications on the Eclipse IDE, you will eventually run them to see if they work like they should. The first thing you will learn is that they will not work if there are errors, as signified by a red X by a line of code. Android has a tool known as *DDMS (Dalvik Debug Monitor Server)* that allows the user to debug on an actual device, instead of using the emulator on Eclipse.

An emulator is like the stage for which an application does rehearsals. I discuss in detail how to set up the emulator on Eclipse in Chapter 12. I have found that running an application on Eclipse and using the emulator on it can take many minutes of loading. In my experience, it's much faster to plug in my own Android device. This way, whenever I run a program on Eclipse, it shows up on my Android device in seconds.

This is how to set up your Android tablet or smartphone for use as an emulator:

1. Make certain that your phone or tablet is recognized by your computer. This means that the proper USB drivers for your Android device are installed and working on your laptop or desktop. For my Droid X phone, the Internet browser opens to a Verizon site every time I plug it in. Just because you can move files from your Android device to your computer doesn't mean your computer recognizes your Android device. Chances are, it just sees a portable memory storage device, and wouldn't know your Android device from a thumb drive. I found that my computer didn't recognize my phone until I downloaded the proper drivers. I simple performed a Google search with Droid X drivers, and was able to find several places to download them.

2. Open Eclipse and choose the Window Android SDK and AVD Manager. You'll see the same screen shown in the last step of installing the Android SDK.

3. Select Available Packages on the left side of the window.

4. If you look at what is available, you will find the USB driver package in the Android repository. It will have Revision listed after it, along with the number of its current version. Select the USB driver package.

5. Click Install Selected at the bottom right of the window.

6. Accept the license and click Install.

7. Close the program after it is done.

8. Exit the Android SDK and AVD Manager.

9. Go into your Android device and click Settings.

10. On this Settings screen, select Applications.

11. On the Application Settings screen, select Development.

12. On the Development screen, check the "USB debugging" option.

Your phone and your computer should now be able to work together to build applications. You should see any application that you build in Eclipse run on your connected Android device.

Summary

The Android application market has recently experienced a high volume of growth in the past few years, and it has shown itself to be a huge competitor of Apple's App Store. However, there are so many Android applications on the market that a developer really has to have something different and outstanding to make good profits. It is important for developers to study the market and determine what versions are best to program their applications in.

Now that you have the tools that you need to succeed as an app developer, you should start thinking about what sort of app you want to make. Yes, that is an obvious step, and you probably already have at least one in mind. We'll discuss this next step in the next chapter. You might want to get yourself prepared by brushing up on Java.

CHAPTER 2

Questions to Ask About Your Android Application

At this point in the book, I am going to cover a lot of subjects that should have a whole book devoted to them. A lot of the finer aspects of programming Android apps are going to be essentially skipped over, during this chapter. As I mentioned in the first chapter, this is not a book about how to program Android applications, but how to market them.

However, I have devoted Chapter 12 to programming in Android, which will aid the Android developer with projects. If you want, you can skip to Chapter 12, read about some tools that will help you program on Eclipse, and then try it out for yourself. If there is one thing that I have learned about creating Android applications, it is that you learn by doing. The more you learn to code, the easier it becomes.

How Android Gives Developers the Tools to Succeed

From a developer's standpoint, one of the best things about working with Android is that you do not have to rewrite new code with every application. There are all sorts of developer's tools to make certain that your application runs its activity or activities well.

Let's say you want an application that can take a picture, and then send that picture with a geotag location all across your social network. It's simple if you are programming with Android. Well, actually, it's not quite simple, but not as difficult as writing all of the programming code yourself.

Android has a lot of widgets—advanced UI elements—that you can use to make your application simple and user-friendly. All of this is done in a basic UI element called a *view*. There are also various other hardware tools that an Android developer should become familiar with in order to create applications that can do more. Examples of these tools include the camera, accelerometer, GPS radio, and proximity sensor.

The Android developer also has the option of grabbing more tools from phone manufacturers themselves. For example, Sony Ericsson has an application known as Timescape that is the central hub for most social activities on its Android phones. The company offers an extension development kit (EDK) so that users can create their own extensions of Timescape, and it is available at the Sony Ericsson site. Obtaining such development kits is often very simple and generally free of charge.

In addition to this, the Android developer should be able to access other application programming interfaces (APIs) in order to allow programs to work together with other programs. There is a terrific list of many of them at http://developer.android.com/reference/packages.html.

So right now, you're probably looking at the Android toolkit like a wide-eyed kid who looks at a large LEGO set. The challenge and the fun is all about finding what you can build, and you are not limited by the amount of pieces. You can also build on some projects that are already constructed. Figure 2-1 is something quick that I was able to use simply by accessing the SDK samples.

Figure 2-1. *The code for a simple Android application that leads to playing the Lunar Lander game, as seen from Eclipse*

The program in Figure 2-1 is Lunar Lander—just one of the sample programs available in the SDK. It is based on a video game that was made by Atari in 1979. That game was made with black-and-white vector graphics, and the player was a spaceship that had to land softly on an alien world. Controls were from left to right, and there was the occasional thrust to slow descent. The challenge was to land in the right space or crash the ship.

If you want to change the game so the lander looks different, or change the sound effects, it is actually a simple matter of altering the code. (Just make certain that you follow the software license that you see in Figure 2-1.)

For example, the Commodore 64 had a similar game in the 1980s called Jupiter Lander with exactly the same premise. You could easily make a version of Jupiter Lander by altering the code. However, you should check on who owns the rights to Jupiter Lander before you release it to the Android Market.

Deciding What to Build

Sure, you could make a new Lunar Lander game and give it a different name. Then you could put it on the Android Market, and you have yourself an Android application!

Of course, this isn't very original, isn't it? You're not going to find someone who is willing to spend $0.99 to go to play a game that hasn't changed much since the 1980s. In fact, a search for "Lunar Lander" on the Android Market reveals two lander games, both of them available for free. If you want to succeed on the Android Market, you are going to have to come up with something a little bit more complex than this.

Of course, there are many Android applications that are based on simplicity that have made a lot of money. For example, I find that one of the most useful apps that I have is a simple flashlight. It seems like every day I find a need for a light, and if I have my Android phone on me, I can do much better than curse the darkness. Color Flashlight (Figure 2-2) does nothing more than cover the screen with one user-defined color of pixels, which creates an illuminating effect. Color Flashlight is not too complex of a program, and it is the simplicity of it that makes it work for Android users (until the battery dies).

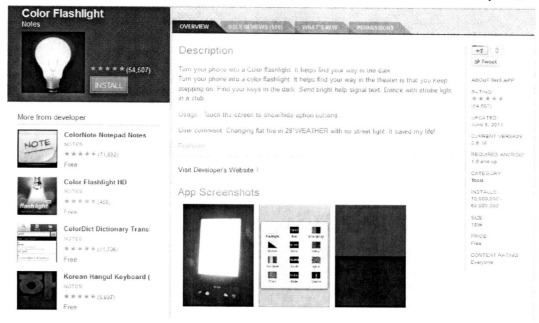

Figure 2-2. *An example of a simple Android application that is useful in many ways. Applications like this make me wish that I had thought of them first.*

If you go into the Android Market and type "flashlight," you will get many results for applications that will essentially do the same as Color Flashlight (some of them can be seen on the left in Figure 2-2). I am not certain who developed the first flashlight app for Android, but I'm certain that it was quickly imitated. The important thing to note is that these flashlight apps do exactly what they are supposed to do (provide light), and many more of them have some extra features. Color Flashlight allows the user to make some hypnotic flashing patterns, and even spell out some text, so users can carry around their own private neon sign.

Special features like these are not too complex to program, and set Android applications apart from other similar ones. Marketing is all about making certain that Android users will find your application, possibly among several similar ones that may or may not be imitators. It is also about presenting your application to users so that it is the one that they want, as opposed to the competition's. Whatever Android application you design should probably be quite simple, but with enough features that will set it apart from whatever competition you'll come across. In short, marketing will put whatever application you have in the proper spotlight so you can sell it to your users.

Creating an Original Application

If you have this book, you may already have a successful app for iOS, and the only reason that you bought the book was to make certain that you can market this iOS app as an Android application. If this is the case, then you have probably learned the hard way that very few (if any) applications are an overnight smash. Here is another fact that you shouldn't have to learn the hard way: even the best marketing cannot take the worst application to anyone's top-ten list.

If you have dabbled in the iOS app arena before, then you should still read this book. There are certain elements of marketing to the iOS crowd that apply to the Android crowd, but other elements that only apply to Android. Whatever your experience is with writing applications, you will want to go through this simple list of questions for Android applications.

What Do You Want Your App to Do?

This is a pretty obvious question, and I'm going to assume that you bought this book because you already have a great idea for an application, and you just want to figure out how you can sell it on the Android Market. In fact, you will discover that the more applications you put out, the more ideas for them you will have.

However, you may be the type of person who wants to get into a lucrative business, but needs some help on the creative side. If you are looking for ideas, the easiest place to start is to think about what you want to see on an Android device. Here are some possible questions of inspiration:

- What hobbies do you have that could be made more fun with an Android application?

- What games do you play that haven't been made into applications already?

- What jobs that you do could be made simpler with an application?

You also might want to ask friends, family, and people in your social networks these questions. Another way of finding ideas is looking at newspapers and magazines.

After all, we should not have to wait for a big company like Microsoft or Google to create software to solve our problems for us. Android gives us the tools to build the solution ourselves. We are now living in an era where technology is getting easier to use, which is turning the average consumer into a competent developer. This is what makes the mobile application marketplace different from the traditional software industry; the small programmer can truly make and market a program that can do something better than a product from the billion-dollar software industry. Best of all, the programmer has the right to take his or her deserved piece of the pie, instead of seeing the great majority of the profits go to giant corporations. While I am on the subject of profits, let me just say this and get it out of the way: Google makes 30 percent of everything that is sold on the Android Market. So for every $0.99 application, Google is getting about $0.30 of that. All right, I'm glad we got that out of the way.

Anyway, the whole mobile application market has changed the way that business is done, and much of it is based on doing complex things in a simple way. Sometimes it is not about creating some grand and original product, but creating a terrific shortcut. The easier you make things for your users, the more they will appreciate you for it.

For example, there is an Android app known as Viewdle SocialCamera (see Figure 2-3) that allows the user to tag friends on their mobile photos and share them directly via Facebook, Flickr, MMS, and e-mail. Without it, users would have to take a picture, upload it to Facebook, and then tag it from their computer. Viewdle SocialCamera allows users to skip a step in the photo-tagging process, and becomes very useful for those who like to tag pictures on their social network.

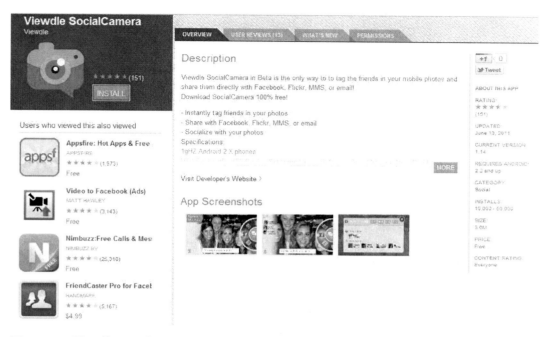

Figure 2-3. *Viewdle SocialCamera provides a way to tag friends from mobile Android phones. It is a good example of how a good Android application doesn't have to be too complex, just a simple time-saver.*

In other words, it is not necessary to reinvent the wheel when coming up with the next great mobile application. Sometimes it is just a matter of creating the vehicle that can put that wheel in better motion. If your Android application can do something in one tap rather than two, then it has a reason for being. Also, have you ever noticed that a lot of iOS applications are not on Android yet? Imagine if you were the one who made it possible!

Now all you have to do is figure out how to use the tools that Android provides to put your idea in motion. Yes, that is the hard part, and if you want to contract someone else to do it on a site such as www.odesk.com/, I don't blame you.

Is the Application Simple to Use?

I have downloaded several scheduling applications for Android that I ended up erasing because they were too complicated to use. Considering that most people often use their Android devices with just one hand, you should figure out how to make your application do as much as possible with just a few finger swipes and very few touchscreen finger touches. I find that speech-to-text is valuable for navigation and texting, so you should probably make certain that feature is available on your application to make it even easier to use.

What makes the aforementioned Color Flashlight application so successful is that it is so simple to use. If it took several swipes to access the flashlight, then I wouldn't use it. As it is, the flashlight is its default setting, with a bright light coming on the moment the icon is activated. The other features are easy to find by clicking the menu button.

You should consider the framework of your program, and make certain that the dumbest user should be able to manipulate the most complex of its features.

What Problem Does Your Android Application Solve?

I'm not saying that your Android application has to make the world a better place, but it had better solve some sort of problem, even if it is just boredom.

You might have seen a recent commercial for Geico insurance where the announcer comes out to a blank stage and says, "Could switching to Geico really save you 15 percent or more on car insurance? Do people use smartphones to do dumb things?"

The ad cuts to three men at an office using their smartphones to make dumb sound effects, pop a virtual bottle of champagne, and use an Android application known as BroStache. As it turns out, BroStache is made by Geico (see Figure 2-4). Talk about marketing one's apps!

The commercial ends with the three geeky guys using their phones as improvised musical instruments. One of them is a guitar, and the other is a trumpet, which sounds like the ever-so-popular fart applications that are on the Market in abundance.

Figure 2-4. Geico's BroStache application for Android. When you hold up your smartphone to your mouth, the virtual mouth moves—proof that people use their smartphones for dumb things.

Yes, there are a lot of applications that do dumb things, and a lot of them actually sell. I'm sure Geico created the app to market its service, as well as have fun. A lot of applications are based on the premise of "quick-fix" entertainment. Not that there is anything wrong with that, because a vast majority of moneymaking applications are based on the temporary relief of boredom. I honestly don't think that Angry Birds makes the world a better place, but sometimes, in the midst of a boring situation, it certainly makes my world a better place!

As a developer, you need to have a ready answer for when someone asks you, "Why did you make this application?" If the answer is not "for fun," then state the problem that your application solves.

Some of the more common types of applications are those that are informational. A lot of companies have figured out that they can take the information that is available on their web site and put it in app form. While a user can simply take out their Android device and examine the web site, it can be difficult to navigate a web site on a device with a small screen. The application allows the company to put all the pertinent information in a smaller package, and give the user exactly what he or she is looking for.

The first application that I designed was for a church. I had been noticing that a lot of big churches were getting applications of their own, and I decided to help out a local church to get one of its own.

These days, there is an app for everything, and most apps are out to solve some sort of problem. I would not be surprised if we were heading to an age where everything had an application, just like everything has a web site. I would also not be surprised if the future revealed a way for end users to turn themselves into applications, just like Facebook and MySpace allow inexperienced computer users to create their own web sites. But for now, companies look to developers to solve the problem of applications.

Who Is Your Target Audience?

Ideally, your product should be used by everyone, but this hardly ever happens in the real world. It usually turns out that there is some group or culture that makes heavy use of a product. Advertisers realize that, and often tailor their commercials or other forms of advertising to this crowd.

Think of how Wheaties uses professional athletes on its boxes. The image of an Olympic-winning competitor on the cereal box shows that the cereal is the "Breakfast of Champions." It is definitely made for the jocks or sports enthusiasts. I'm sure that you have noticed that a lot of tech products are targeted to the "geek" crowd, as are video games and comic book–adapted movies.

In other words, there is probably a specific type of audience—whether it be scrapbookers, stamp collectors, sports nuts, or any other type of group—who would be more likely to buy your Android application than the average consumer.

This is the most important question to consider when marketing your Android application, and a great factor in determining your personal marketing plan. In addition to finding your audience, it is also important to find your culture as well. There is a lot more to culture than meets the eye, so I have devoted the entire next chapter to discussing it. It might help you answer the next important question.

What Category Will This Application Go Under?

I have a Droid X phone, and when I go to the Android Market, I can select three specific icons underneath the slideshow. They are Apps, Games, and Verizon. If I select Apps, the Categories list will appear, and I can select a category. At the time of writing, they are

- All applications
- Books & Reference
- Business
- Comics
- Communication
- Education
- Entertainment
- Finance
- Health & Fitness

- Lifestyle
- Live Wallpaper
- Media & Video
- Medical
- Music & Audio
- News & Magazines
- Personalization
- Photography
- Productivity
- Shopping
- Social
- Sports
- Tools
- Transportation
- Travel & Local
- Weather
- Widgets
- Libraries & Demo

I won't describe them individually, but your application is probably going to have to fall into one of these categories unless some other one is made. If you need clarification on what these categories are, then I suggest looking at each of them and studying the applications there. One of the problems with the categories is they are deliberately vague in their descriptions. Also, you will be stuck with whatever description you pick, as you can't share a category.

Viewdle is listed under Social, but it could just as easily be listed under Photography. Personally, I think it is better listed under Social, because the purpose of the application is to make social networking easier.

Sometimes it is difficult to tell what category to choose for your application. Do you put a good game in Entertainment or Gaming? Do you put your learning application in Books & References or Education? It is really about where you think your target audience will find it, and what the purpose of your application is. In the end, you really have to decide who your audience is, and what purpose they will use your application for. Then you can make the choice for your category.

Has Someone Already Done This Before?

This one is a little bit difficult to tell. For example, let's say that you wanted to make an app that can organize baseball cards by team, year, and so on. How in the world can you tell whether someone has already done that?

Sure, you can go into the Android Market and do a search on "baseball card organizer." I suppose that is as good as a description as any, but I checked, and there is nothing matching it. You will find a lot of search results if you just use "baseball cards."

By the way, just because someone has done your idea doesn't mean that you can't do the same thing, but better! There have been a lot of successful businesses and entertainment franchises that have succeeded this way. After all, where would Facebook be today without MySpace? Where would the TV show *Glee* be without the TV movie *High School Musical*? Where would *Twilight* be without other vampire genre stories? In those examples, it is about doing something that someone has done before, but in a more original way.

Be warned. You had better make certain that your app really has at least a few new or better features than your competitor, or you will be ignored. That is a worst-case scenario; the best case is you will be mocked. If you are mocked, people might download your Android application out of sheer morbid curiosity. If you are ignored, though, no one wants to download what you have, so you will lose business.

This is not to say that you can't get a little profit from being an imitator. However, trying to make money by jumping onto someone else's coattails involves fly-by-night operations in order to maximize one's profits, possibly before any legal action gets taken, if you are using plagiarist strategies. I discuss how to legally protect your application later, but you definitely want to do everything you can to avoid a lawsuit!

My best advice is do your homework. My second best advice is do your homework again. Although everyone is unique, there are generally at least two people doing the same thing at any given time. Therefore, you want to check to see how many Android applications, or applications on other platforms, will be competing with what you have to offer. So, when you search for your "new" application on the Android Market, use every variation of keywords that you can. If nothing else, this will help you to figure out what keywords can be used to find your Android application, which will come in handy when marketing it.

By the way, you will probably notice that when you do your search, certain applications appear at the top of the list. As you might have guessed, this is not a randomly ordered list. There are specific reasons why Color Flashlight appears at the top in a search for "flashlight." Chances are, the apps that hit the top of your list will be the highest-rated applications of their type, and they will be your stiffest competition.

In addition to your searches on the Android Market, you also might want to look at some third-party markets to see what is popular on the Android platform:

- *AndroLib* (www.androlib.com/): Not only will AndroLib give you an excellent search engine capable of finding Android applications and games, but it offers statistics, news, and a forum about the Android Market. It also has a Top of the Day chart with both the free apps and paid apps, and a scoreboard for applications and developers.

- *Amazon* (www.amazon.com/mobile-apps/b/ref=topnav_storetab_mas?ie=UTF8&node=2350149011): As I mentioned in Chapter 1, it is possible for Android developers to submit their applications to the Amazon Appstore. In addition to this, the Appstore for Android has other resources that will show developers what applications are the most popular, including their bestsellers, top-rated apps, new releases, and free apps. It also has a place to search for specific categories of applications.

- *AndroidZoom* (www.androidzoom.com/): According to its FAQ section, "AndroidZoom.com is the place where Android users may discover and download the best Android apps for their devices." It also has reviews and recommendations, and sorts them by categories as well. It also has the "hottest Android applications" including free, paid, and on-sale apps.

- *Appaware.org* (https://market.android.com/details?id=org.appaware): This is a terrific site for finding trending applications on the Android Market. Applications are organized into categories, with tags. It is also an Android application, so it can be an application for finding applications!

- *AppBrain* (www.appbrain.com/): This page allows the user to discover the best Android applications by search, rank, and category. It also enables the user to install and manage these apps directly from the web and share them on your phone with your friends.

- *Aproov* (www.aproov.com/): This site is in beta, but it advertises itself as "the way an app store was meant to be." It has its applications organized into very precise categories, but there are no top or "most popular" lists. It is made for developers, and there is a specific place to upload and manage your apps.

- *Appsfire* (http://appsfire.com/): This site is dedicated to helping users "discover and enjoy mobile applications." Appsfire even has an app that you can get for free, and its official site has an "AppTrends" section that informs the user of the most popular apps on Facebook.

- *doubleTwist* (www.doubletwist.com/): This company has a unique vision of creating "a unifying media platform that connects consumers with all their media and all their devices, regardless of whether they are online or offline." You will find a lot of applications here.

- *GetJar* (www.getjar.com/): GetJar is "the world's largest free app store," and distributes more than 150,000 mobile applications for a variety of operating systems. It has over 2 billion downloads, and it has lists of top and new applications as well. As with Amazon, you can get your application put on GetJar if you apply.

- *MobiHand* (www.mobihand.com/): According to its site, MobiHand is "a leading distributor of software and content for smartphones," and this company partners with media companies, portals, retailers, device manufacturers, and operators in order to deliver "customized desktop and on-device app shops." It has more on its store than just Android, but if you go to OnlyAndroid (http://onlyandroid.mobihand.com/), you can see what they have exclusively for Android. The user can browse the store in order to find popular applications and search by category.

- *SlideME* (http://slideme.org/): SlideME has a different approach to its Android application store, as it provides applications for niche markets, based on geographic location. It also has "types of applications that users can't find in traditional channels." Additionally, it has a popularity list, category list, and a search engine.

What Are You Going to Call Your Application?

"What's in a name?" That Shakespeare guy could have been talking about naming your Android application when he said that "a rose by any other name would smell as sweet." In the same manner, it isn't always necessary to name your application the obvious one. The true test of a name is discovering one that is catchy and memorable.

I'm sure you are all familiar with Google, a company name that we commonly use a verb today. Before we were all "googling" stuff we wanted to know more about, we never used the word *Google* in a sentence. The name supposedly is derived from the word googolplex, a number that is followed by a googol zeroes. A googol (pronounced the same as *Google*) is the numerical value of 1 followed by 100 zeroes. The Googleplex is also the name of the headquarters of Google.

I suppose that Google implies a vast number and complications, but even that has very little to do with what Google is most known for, which is its search engine. Google could have chosen "WebSearcher" or "Seekers" for its name, as those would have been descriptive. In the online world, many names are chosen so users will not mix up the company with another. In fact, there are entire companies, such as Interbrand, devoted to naming things to make sure that proposed names are unique don't translate to something bad in another language.

It is less important what the name is as long as it denotes a brand—a way that a company differentiates its goods or services from others. Google is a good example of a successful brand. Before I discuss branding any more, let me add an important piece of trivia about Google's name. Google announced on April 1, 2010 that it was changing its name to "Topeka." As you can see by the date of the announcement, it was an April Fool's Day prank. In all honesty, if the company had originally chosen the name Topeka, and used similar marketing strategies, we would be "Topeka-ing" things. As it stands right now, Google is a brand, and it would be a mistake for a company as big as Google to suddenly change its name.

If you don't believe me, here's an example. You might know of a big fast-food company known as Jack in the Box. In 1985, the company decided that it wanted to remove the juvenile association with a toy and go for a classier image with the name of Monterey Jack's. It was a colossal failure, and the company brought back its name in 1986. I bring this up to demonstrate the danger of rebranding, and how naming creates a standard that cannot be changed very easily.

Another example of a successful brand is Apple. The name Apple has nothing to do with computers, but the company has done so much in the past few decades that it is an internationally known brand, like Google.

This is the challenge of picking a name. One would think that the most descriptive names would be the best choices, since they are the ones that will turn up on search engines. However, many descriptive names are not protectable against trademark infringements. I will discuss trademarks later in this chapter.

As an Android developer, it is important that you come up with a name that will describe what your application does without going into too much detail. This will make it show up on search engines. Earlier I discussed an application that can organize baseball cards. If I called it Baseball Card Organizer, then I can guarantee it would be difficult to trademark. That name is too descriptive, and it is also way too long. Considering that the Android Market only shows a certain amount of letters, the full name of the app will be cut off. I could call it BC Organizer, but I would have to market that well so people will know what "BC" stands for. BC Organizer could easily refer to organizing events that happened in years BC, for example.

If you want to pick a name that has nothing to do with your product, then you are going to have to do a lot of marketing to make certain people know about it. However, if the name has at least something to do with what your product does and is easy to remember, it helps.

I recently discovered an application known as Thrutu, which allows two Android phone users to share location, contacts, and photos (see Figure 2-5). The name *Thrutu* means nothing standing on its own, but, after using the application, it implies that I am sending things through to another Android user. In short, the name is a descriptor if you know the product.

Figure 2-5. Thrutu, an Android application with a short and descriptive name, provided you know what it does

Your job as a developer is to find a name that is a balance of originality and a sensible description of what the application does, if possible. Keep in mind that there is a limit to the amount of letters you can use. If your name is too long, it could get cut off when displayed on the Android Market. It is best to go with one original word that is simple to remember. An original word is less likely to have already been used, and marketing will help that word become your personal brand.

Also, to avoid lawsuits, do a quick search on the US Patent and Trademark Office's Trademark Electronic Search System (TESS). Just go to http://uspto.gov/trademarks/ (or the equivalent sites for any other countries that you want to market to outside the United States). The last thing you want to do is market an Android application that has the same trademarked name as something already out there. I'll go more into detail about trademarks a little later in this chapter.

Once you have your name down, you should definitely snatch it up as a domain name for the web site devoted to your application. Yes, it is important that you have a web site, and yes, I will go more into detail about it in the next chapter.

Search the Whois database to discover if your name has been taken as a URL. Just go to http://whois.net and type in your particular domain name, along with the suffix (.com, .org, .net, or whatever). If you find that it has been taken, you can add something to the name or insert a hyphen in the name, but only if you are certain that your web site will not be mistaken for this other web site. You don't want to get your application mixed up with another one, as that publicity you'll get from this is temporary and dependent on how popular the other application is. The worst-case scenario is that you buy a domain name that is similar to a porn site or some other site that represents some questionable business.

Where Do You Want Your Application to Run

Just like certain applications for iOS are optimized for the iPad, you should consider whether your particular application might be good for Android tablets, and whether you should ignore the smartphone platforms entirely. With the larger screen and other features of Honeycomb, you might consider programming your application in Android 3.0.

Keep in mind that Android 3.0 isn't on many devices yet (at the time of writing), so it might be better to go with a lower version, such as Android 1.6, Considering that Boost Mobile stores are full of lower versions of Android, it might be better to program your application for these types of smartphones instead of the latest model of Android. This could give you access to a greater audience than the Honeycomb Android crowd.

Now, there are some applications that play well on certain phones. For example, certain games play particularly well on the Sony Ericsson Xperia PLAY (also known as the PlayStation Phone), but not on other phones. So that super-cool gaming application that you're planning might do well there, but could be limited on other devices.

It is important that you do your research as a developer and find out what devices will play well for your application. This will change the way you market your application, and help you find a more specific audience.

What You Need to Do, Legally, As an Application Developer

Okay, let's say you were able to make that Android application. Now you should know that your Android application is your personal intellectual property, which means that you or your company has "intangible rights" to your creative work. Knowing your personal intellectual property rights can protect you from imitators who are out to get a quick buck from your application. For example, if someone steals your icon, graphics, or idea, knowing your rights could help you file an appropriate lawsuit to recover from the theft of your intellectual property.

What sort of rights do you want? You want something that can be obtained as quickly and accurately as possible in order to protect your investment. As you know, Android applications can be created in a very short period of time, and with new versions of Android coming out approximately every six months, it is difficult to see where the market is headed.

This last section of the chapter provides a summary of what to do to protect yourself legally. It is based on Chapter 3 of *The Business of iPhone and iPad App Development*, by Dave Wooldridge and Michael Schneider (Apress, 2011). (Michael Schneider, who wrote Chapter 3, is a successful lawyer and app-maker). All quotes are taken from his work.

Copyrights

A copyright is when a writer is granted "the right to dictate who can copy, distribute, publicly perform, modify, or create derivative works from their original work of authorship." In legal terms, the moment that you put your pen to the paper, or start typing, copyright protection is automatically granted. Copyright can protect things like source code, graphics, sound effects, and other creative works you put in your application, but it does not protect any facts or ideas that are not used in a creative or artistic way.

Obtaining a copyright can give you a base level of protection that would come in handy when suing an obvious imitator of your ideas. The emphasis in that last sentence would be *obvious*, as copyright protection can extend to cases when your competitor is stealing graphics from the icon or the application itself, but does not apply when an imitator's application is merely based on the same underlying idea as yours.

The current filing fee is about $65, but it can be lower ($35) if filed online. You can file online at www.copyright.gov/eco/, and get a lot of your questions answered in the tutorial at www.copyright.gov/eco/eco-tutorial.pdf.

Trademarks

Now let's talk about trademarks. Trademarks are intended to keep others from confusing your company with anyone else. A trademark does not protect a concept or idea, but it will protect your name and logo. In today's market, logos and icons are crucial. Think about companies like McDonald's, Microsoft, and, for the sake of argument, Google's Android division. No doubt images of their logos come to mind—the golden arches, the Windows symbol, and that green robot guy, respectively.

Trademark rights are like copyright rights: they go into effect the moment you use a name or symbol as an identifier for the source of your Android application. However, you might want to get better protection by filing a trademark registration with the US Patent and Trademark Office, in case you ever need to pursue a trademark action to federal court. You can find out more at http://uspto.gov.

Protecting Your Trade Secrets

In developing your own personal intellectual property, there are some things that you probably wouldn't divulge to the average person. I know that as a professional blogger, I don't state my business contacts on my individual blog posts, and I have strategies that I don't share with everyone. This is why there is trade-secret law.

There are various ways of protecting trade secrets. If you have people working for you or with you on your Android application, then they need to know the importance of keeping all their information on private drives and servers, and it probably wouldn't hurt to ask them to sign confidentiality agreements, also known as nondisclosure agreements (NDAs).

Is a Patent Right for You?

Now that I've briefly discussed the laws of copyright, patents, and trademarks, let's go into patents. A patent grants an inventor the right to stop other people from using, making, or exporting the subject of an invention. It is not recommended that most Android developers get their own patents, as obtaining one is an extremely costly venture.

If you have an application that you know will be pertinent in the next few years, and will seriously change things, then a patent might be the way to go. However, the average patent costs about $10,000, and in order to obtain one, your invention must be "new and useful, and you must be able to describe it in a way that would allow a person reasonably skilled in the invention's area to make the invention work."

Another option is the provisional patent application, for which you can send a basic description of your invention to the patent office to establish an early effective filing date if you wish to file a full patent application on the invention itself. It is pretty weak as far as legally enforceable rights are concerned, but it gives you the right to use that "patent-pending" term that you see attached to many product ads. In case you are wondering what it means, it tells potential competitors that there is a patent application in the works on your product and/or service. You can file for a provisional patent application online through this web site: https://efs.uspto.gov/efile/portal/efs-unregistered.

Summary

Android is really giving developers the tools to succeed, and there are even more tools available from the phone manufacturers themselves. Your job is to come up with an application that people need and is simple to use. You need to know what category your app will fit into and who your target audience will be. You should also check to see if someone else is doing what your application is doing, just so you know who the competition is. This information is going to come in useful when naming your application as well. There are some legal aspects that you should take care of. You should protect your intellectual property rights as appropriate with a copyright, trademark, or even a patent.

CHAPTER 3

You're Not Selling an Application, You're Selling a Culture

Hopefully, you have answered all my questions about your Android applications that were laid out in Chapter 2. For the sake of argument, let's say that you have a good start on the Android application itself. If you haven't, then I will give you something else that you can think about while you are constructing the next hit Android application.

I never like to make promises that I can't keep, so let's talk about how much money you will probably make. It probably won't be a lot, at least not at first. If you go to the Android Market, you will find that a lot of applications that have been abandoned by developers. You can usually tell because there have only been 50 to 100 downloads, a sign that the application may have tried to capitalize on a trend that peaked too soon. That, or the developer tried to do too much and put out an application that was shoddy, and the application received too many bad reviews. In other words, the developer was probably hoping to put his or her application out on the Market in order to make a quick buck. This is a short-term goal, and although you might make some money, it won't last long.

Think about the applications that are huge successes. Start by thinking of the ones that have passed the test of time, for any platform. This can be difficult, as the mobile application world isn't even a decade old, to this writing. I can think of a few applications that have made their mark, like Dropbox, Evernote, Pandora, Shazam, Google Googles, and Barcode Scanner, as well as other gaming/entertainment applications like Angry Birds and Cut the Rope.

Perhaps it would be better to think about any software that has made its mark. I'm sure that we all use programs from Microsoft, Google, Adobe, and other programs from billion-dollar software companies on a daily basis.

Let me take a giant step in this illustration and ask you to think about anything that has been a huge success. I'm talking about Wal-Mart, McDonalds, Lady Gaga, or Oprah. What these companies and celebrities sell isn't their products, it is a culture.

The Definition of Culture

Culture is one of those words that is overused, and most dictionaries will give you over ten different definitions of it. For our purposes, I am going to use the definition that applies to "the behaviors and beliefs characteristic to a particular group." I'm referring to the definition of culture that people use when they talk about "the youth culture" or "the music culture" or "the coffee shop culture."

Even that definition is very vague, so let me give you another example. Go to the magazine racks at a bookstore or library. You'll see titles like *Forbes, Ebony, Sunset, Rolling Stone, Redbook, Vogue,* and many others. Take out a single issue and look at its ads and articles. Ask yourself what sort of audience this magazine is catering for. What makes a Cosmo girl? Who is a GQ man?

Chances are, the most successful magazines have been in the business for decades, and they have refined their target audiences over the years. Now their target audience is safely in the crosshairs. For long-time readers, the magazine has nothing to do with the information or products that it holds within their pages. What really sells is an idea—some belief that people want to make their own—that the glossy mag brings.

Think about why Facebook has made an impact. It has nothing to do with what it does. In fact, what it does has been done before. It wasn't really about a software program, it was really about relationships. Friends can get together and freely share photos and beliefs, with "like" or "dislike." Facebook is so much of a culture that it has become part of our mass culture. This particular culture states, as its fundamental idea, that all of our friends can be with us in one place, and we can all get along together.

All that from a simple online program. As you might have seen in the movie *The Social Network*, the creators themselves didn't really see where this idea would take them.

Foursquare has a similar strategy. It knows that we can't be with all of our friends all at once, but it at least allows us to keep track of them and find out what they are doing. Foursquare is an extremely popular application on Android and other platforms, and it definitely has a social aspect that has created its own culture.

I didn't tackle this question of culture in the last chapter, as it is difficult to put into a sentence. The question involves finding your target audience, and figuring out how they can truly use their product until it becomes a part of their lives. I suppose that I could phrase that question like this: "What kind of culture does your application bring to users?"

What you need to do is think of your application from a Don Draper point of view. If you are not familiar with that name, then you might want to catch an episode of *Mad Men*. On that popular AMC TV series, Don Draper and his ad agency, Sterling Cooper, are presented with an idea that they must market. Many episodes consist of Don in front of his assistants, thinking out loud about what the idea of the product really means.

For example, there was an episode where Kodak was wanting Sterling Cooper to advertise its newest invention, the slide projector. After trying out the project, Don concludes that the purpose of the projector is to provide a way of traveling through memories like a child, which is why he calls the circular tray holder the Carousel.

History reveals that the Carousel didn't get its name from Don Draper, but I hope you see the point that I am making: it's usually not about what the product can do, but what the user believes it will do. This belief is what will determine the culture of your application.

Defining Your Culture

I mentioned before how failed or discontinued apps often have short-term goals attached to them, which might explain why they aren't still being sold. As a developer, you have to think about the long-term plan. Instead of hoping that your app will be a success, come up with a plan that will make it a success. You want to create an application that will create its own culture, and thus become a part of our mass culture. I'll have more to say about a marketing plan in Chapter 4, but let me briefly touch on a how to come up with the culture for your application.

It doesn't matter if you can't program your app to do everything that you dreamed it could on the day that it launches. Chances are, you have already discovered how difficult programming is, and the technology may not even exist yet to have your application do exactly what you want it to do. That's fine—as long as you can make a program that can at least do some of it, that might be enough to justify a download by an Android user. Remember what I said in Chapter 2, that sometimes it is about making an application that will allow a user to do something easier, which usually means fewer steps involved in implementation.

For example, let's say that you have an application that serves as a universal remote. First of all, let me tell you that a lot of other applications that are doing this, and it usually involves another piece of hardware to get it to work. So you really need to make sure it can at least replicate the basic features of your competition before you release it to the Android Market.

Now, what kind of culture can you present with this? That all depends on what you can offer users, especially if there are features that your competitors don't offer. It would be helpful to look into the future of home theater electronics to see where your product can go. For example, if you can create a universal remote that can deal with set-top boxes like the Roku or even video game systems, then you might have something that your competitors don't have. Combine that with some cloud computing and a DVR, and you've really got a package that you can offer customers!

So what kind of culture are you creating? Your target audience is definitely the home theater crowd—but don't just give them a product, give them something to believe in. Show them that by using your Android application they are transporting themselves into "a world of their own." I'll leave you to decide whether or not that is a decent slogan, but you see what I am getting at: you are showing a belief for your target audience to rally around.

Creating a Style That Is Unique

I will have to admit that I am the least conscious when it comes to fashion and other trends, but there is one thing that I think we all know about, and that is style. Like culture, the word has many definitions, but I am referring to the basic appearance of an application, not to mention what it says about the application itself.

Let me take a moment to speak to those who are coming up with gaming applications, which is a very popular type of application now. In fact, you will see from many of the Android application rating sites mentioned in Chapter 2 that several-best selling apps are gaming ones. It is important to get the game play right in your game, but the gaming applications that really take off are the ones that present their games with style.

Think about the surrealistic puzzle game Myst in the early 1990s, or the apocalyptic art-deco influence of Bioshock from the last decade. Why did those games create such a phenomenon? The designers created a world that was uniquely its own, and the unique style of this world completely sucked gamers in. Even a simple game like Angry Birds has a sense of style behind it, with its bright colors and minimalist simplicity. There's something about these games that creates a world separate from us. Not only do they create a world that we can practically live in, but they make us willing to trade in our real-life problems to experience problems that exist there. Most games bring us an idea that shows that we can overcome any problem with a lot of determination. This is the culture, and it is done with style.

The same principle of style in gaming applies to movies. Film franchises like *The Matrix*, *Star Wars*, *Lord of the Rings*, and *Harry Potter* all have very particular styles. Even films that don't take place in fantastic worlds still have a genuine style, such as the nostalgic '60s look of *Catch Me If You Can*, or the quirky suburban looks of indie films like *Juno* and *Napoleon Dynamite*. From the sets to the music to the costumes, it doesn't take an expert to see when something doesn't belong in a film. You know it when you see it. Can you imagine if you saw pastel colors in the world of *The Matrix*? An iPod being used by Gollum from *Lord of the Rings*? What about Harry Potter with a gun? None of these examples would have been considered for the styles of these movies.

In the same way, everything in your application has to fit together in a seamless fashion to create a unique look. This includes the icon, logo, and the user interface (UI).

The Icon

There used to be a dandruff shampoo that had the slogan "You never get a second chance to make a first impression." Cliché as that is, it is very true.

One of the toughest things about marketing an Android application is just making sure that people even know about it. You'll see how to solve that problem in later chapters, but let's say that someone is looking at the Android Market and has found your application. What is it that they see? Along with the name of your application, design company, rating, and cost, there is the first impression in visual form: the icon. Even though "you can't judge a book by its cover," the fact is that most people do. Not only that, they look to the icon and hope to get some idea as to what the application does.

This is definitely something to think about as you are deciding what you want your icon to look like. That icon is more than just the square that the user taps to access your application; it is the symbol of your application. You know how I have been saying that you are selling a culture? I am going to briefly talk about another definition of culture that defines a group of people. Notice that most cultures, such as tribes, countries, and companies, have a symbol, such as a flag. Groups have a way of creating a flag and pledging allegiance to it. In Chapter 2, I explained how a name is important, as it creates a brand. People are quick to latch onto brands, so let your icon be that brand.

Your chosen icon should epitomize the functionality of your application. Take the icon from the company Waze (see Figure 3-1), for example. Note the happy face, which is, for lack of a better word, iconic. You'll then notice that the smiley face isn't on a yellow circle, but a dialogue balloon, like the type in most comic panels. You'll then notice that the dialogue balloon has wheels. You may even notice the curvy lines beside the balloon, which is an international indicator that it is getting a signal. The sun is also out, which signifies a nice day outside. Also notice that its smile isn't a mouth, but something that you might see on a U-Turn sign.

Figure 3-1. The official icon for Waze, a social navigation application. This picture says more than a thousand words.

What will a first-time user glean from this simple drawing? This happy dialogue balloon is taking a leisurely trip—but it is not alone, it is connected. This conjures up the culture that Waze is selling: it is "a free social traffic and navigation app that uses real-time road reports from drivers nearby to save commuting time and improve your everyday driving." Even though this description (based on its actual description on the Android Market) isn't completely conveyed by the picture, it is enough to give a potential user a hint of what it actually is.

Waze is an example of a creative approach to what your application does. However, most applications are so simple that they can be summed up in less than the thousand words that a picture can say. For example, if you are creating a gaming application called Zombie Baseball, just have a picture of a zombie holding a baseball bat. You can decide for yourself whether it is better to see the full zombie body at bat, or just a skeletal hand clutching a bat. There is an actual application from Halfbrick known as Age of Zombies that uses the icon in Figure 3-2.

Figure 3-2. The icon for Age of Zombies. This gives you a sample of what you are getting with this game.

As you can see in Figure 3-2, this dinosaur is partly skeletal, which means he is a zombie dinosaur. This means that you are facing a game with zombie dinosaur enemies, which are quite unusual video game foes. In all honesty, this image would have been my first choice for an icon for a game that involves such odd undead foes.

Chances are, you'll probably come up with several ideas for an icon, and have to select just one. Figure 3-3 is another example of an obvious icon. It comes from a gaming application known as Alchemy, which is my current addiction. The game involves mixing elements (which appear to the user as icons) together to form new things. Considering the obvious association with traditional alchemy is the use of potions, why wouldn't you use a beaker like this for an icon?

Figure 3-3. The icon for Alchemy, a gaming application. I can't imagine what you would use for an icon other than this.

When deciding on a look for your icon, it helps to look at what your competition is doing. Please note that you don't want to imitate what your competitors are doing; instead, always try to figure out what they have not thought of yet. You definitely don't want to reproduce copyrighted images, as that will lead to a lawsuit. You want to create something as new as possible, and you will want to study your competition to make certain that your icon doesn't bear too much resemblance to theirs.

Another important aspect of designing an icon for an Android application is that you follow the proper procedure. Just go to http://developer.android.com/guide/practices/ui_guidelines/icon_design.html, and you can download the Icon Templates Pack, which is good for versions of Android 2 and above. The Android Developer guidelines recommend that you use a large artboard to make your icon (preferably an

864×864) artboard. Just to let you know, your icon is going to grow or shrink depending on the screen density that you have. Table 3-1 demonstrates what size your icon will be in certain situations.

Table 3-1. What Size Your Icon Will Be on an Android Device

Icon Type	Low-Density Screen	Medium-Density Screen	High-Density Screen
Launcher	36×36 px	48×48 px	72×72 px
Menu	36×36 px	48×48 px	72×72 px
Status bar on Android 2.3 and later	12w×19h px (preferred; width may vary)	16w×25h px (preferred; width may vary)	24w×38h px (preferred; width may vary)
Status bar on Android 2.2 and below	19×19 px	25×25 px	38×38 px
Tab	24×24 px	32×32 px	48×48 px
Dialog	24×24 px	32×32 px	48×48 px
List view	24×24 px	32×32 px	48×48 px

For additional help, you might want to head to the Android Asset Studio for icon generators (http://android-ui-utils.googlecode.com/hg/asset-studio/dist/index.html), which allows users to quickly and easily generate icons from existing images, clip art, or text.

Now, here is the tricky part. Can you match the style of your icon to look like the rest of your application graphics? For example, if you choose red and black for the colors of your icon, then you should probably feature those colors predominantly in your app. Having a unified style also helps with such "trivial details" as your logo.

Logo

Now that you have an icon that your idea can gather around, you should put some thought into your logo. This may seem insignificant, but think about some of the films that you have watched and remember how the title was written—for example, how old horror films use a creepy, wavy effect on the letters in their titles. If you want more examples, just look through a pile of DVD or Blu-ray movies, and you will see that the way the title is written is as important as the image shown on the case.

A more creative example is *Ghostbusters*, which actually used its iconic image in the logo—but I will leave it up to you to decide whether or not it is a good marketing strategy to use your logo on your icon. The size changes that I discussed earlier might reduce your logo to something unreadable.

Sometimes, you can find a logo by just typing out your app name in a word-processing program, highlighting it, and then playing with fonts. Chances are, you are going to find a style that fits with the culture that your application conveys. If you need some help with that, you can go to several sites that are full of fonts for you to use:

- Dafont (www.dafont.com)

- 1001 Free Fonts (www.1001freefonts.com)

- Urbanfonts (www.urbanfonts.com)

- Myfonts (http://new.myfonts.com)

A little warning on the use of fonts in your logo. I have seen people "borrow" logos before when trying to create a certain look. For example, if I were trying to do a game that resembled Tron, it would be a simple matter of using the same font as that of the movie poster. It is quite simple to find this font (or any other font) online. This font-borrowing technique usually comes off as second rate at best. It generally looks like you're trying to piggyback on someone else's success. Chances are, if someone is trying to play a game that is like Tron, they will download the official application associated with it. Borrowing a font is banking on a user's predisposition to a similar font, and you don't want to come off looking like a copycat.

User Interface

And now I will discuss something that will cost you many hours of programming: the UI. I mentioned in Chapter 2 that you should make your application easy to use, but you should also consider the style of your UI.

Now, you could get to the Android Market with a plain-looking icon, logo, and UI, and you would have . . . a plain-looking application. You should also consider how an Android user might look at your application's screenshots on the Android Market. If he or she finds a similar application that has a better look to it, then you can probably guess which one will get downloaded.

You have probably written down an idea of what sort of menu you are going to have. Chances are, your application is going to have some sort of menu screen the moment the application is opened. You should put in some thought about the style that this menu will have. As an example, Figure 3-4 shows the menu screen for Pulse, a news application that "takes your favorite web sites and transforms them into a colorful and interactive mosaic."

Figure 3-4. The UI for Pulse. Note how easy it is to use and how it makes use of graphics.

Notice the menu up on top, which lists Home, Design, Tech, Art, and Social. From there, it is easy to scroll to see which articles are worth reading.

Like Pulse, you want to create a decent UI that is simple to use and conveys a lot of information in a small space. If you need some help creating one, then you might consider some type of prototyping process so you can see what the UI will eventually look like. There are several ways to do this.

If you are interested in some GUI (graphical user interface) wireframe or mockup programs, there are many available online, including the following:

- *Android GUI Prototyping (www.artfulbits.com/products/free/#Introduction_1)*: This requires Microsoft B Visio B 2003 or higher, and you should be able to access its unique stencils.

- *DroidDraw (www.droiddraw.org/)*: This is a designer/editor/builder for cell phone and tablet application programming on the Android platform. It even has an Android application that allows you to download GUIs from DroidDraw and preview them on an Android device.

- *Pencil (http://pencil.evolus.vn/en-US/Home.aspx)*: Designed by the Pencil Project, this is designed to be a "free and open source tool for making diagrams and GUI prototyping that everyone can use." It appears to only work on the Firefox browser.

You can also get software for a mockup, including some associated with Photoshop. Here are a couple examples:

- *Android GUI PSD (www.matcheck.cz/androidguipsd/)*: This is a Photoshop file with elements of the Android 1.5 GUI to help the open source community with application mockups.

- *Fireworks template for Android (http://unitid.nl/2009/11/fireworks-template-for-android/)*: This has Android UI elements that have been redrawn as vector images. Most elements have been labeled according to the Android vocabulary.

Even though we live in an age where everything is going digital, pencil and paper is still the best way to flush out our ideas. Fortunately, there are a lot of places you can go to get some stencils for Android devices, and one of them is

- *Android Wireframe Templates (http://gliderguns.files.wordpress.com/2010/01/android_wireframe_templates3.pdf)*: This includes some samples of outlines of major Android phones, including the HTC Dream, HTC Hero, HTC Magic, HTC Tattoo, HTC Nexus One, and Motorola Droid.

However, you might want to consider creating an interface that is completely original. This is where you can go really crazy and do something like a funky style of pop-up book, or something that is more than just the usual bundle of buttons, pull-up menus, and finger swipes.

Keep in mind that you want your UI to be consistent with your application's style. You don't want to have a startup menu that is one style, and then have the rest of the application be another one. Your goal is to have an application that is consistent throughout.

Your Application's Web Site

As cool as your application is going to be, it really is rather limited. One of the things that you will learn as a developer is that the less memory an application takes, the better. The challenge is how to take what memory you have to work with and make something of good quality and with many features. That is definitely a programming skill, but if you can't find space for something in your application, why not put it on the official web site?

Since entire books have been written about web site construction, I see no point in going into detail about how to create a cool web site. If you're thinking that there is no wrong way to do a web site, then you're mistaken. I'm sure that you have been to cobweb sites that are full of broken links, and look like they have been long since abandoned by their creators. Yes, the Web is full of sites that have their "newest" content dating back several years ago.

The first thing that you should know about creating a web site is it takes time, and I am not talking about the initial creation. I mean the upkeep that must be done on a daily basis to ensure that the content is fresh. If visitors find that the content is not consistently updated, they are less inclined to return.

In addition to having a web site that is full of timely material, you definitely want to have a web site that matches the style of what you are doing on your application. Here is where you will implement your icon, logo, and many other stylistic aspects of your application. You might want to go to the Android Market and select an application. Under each of them should be a link to the developer's web site, which will often be the official web site of the application. Go on and click on a few for yourself so you can see what they look like. For example, Figure 3-5 shows the Waze web site.

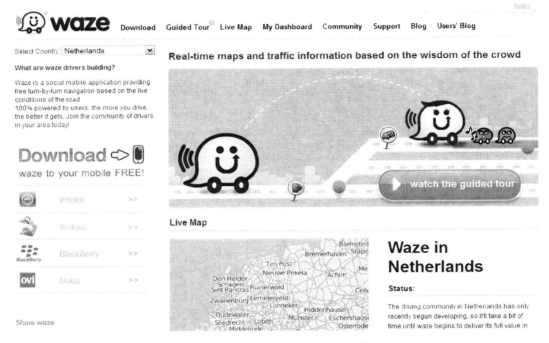

Figure 3-5. This is official web site for Waze. It has a lot more to offer than its mobile application.

In many cases, an Android application is just a mobile version of the site. Its sole purpose is to draw the user to the site itself, where the "real action" takes place. In other cases, the web site feels like something that was developed as an afterthought, when the developer realized that he or she was going to need one.

Let's take a closer look at one example of a developer's web site. You can see that most of these have a blog, community, and much more. Your application is your culture, and your web site is essentially your clubhouse.

The web site is probably the very place where you will first introduce your application, and people could discover what you are doing there. Notice that I say "could," as most web sites are not discovered by accident. Yes, it will probably take some marketing and spreading the word so that people will learn that your site is out there. I'll get to that in other chapters, but let's talk about the next step.

Setting Up Your Web Site

The first thing that you will need for setting up a web site is a domain name. Hopefully, you can ensure that it is the same as your application's name. I have already covered some of that in Chapter 2, under the question of "What will you call your application?"

Once you have your unique URL picked out, you will need to find a web hosting service. You could go with GoDaddy.com, Google Sites, or other such ventures, and you should expect to pay a monthly fee. From there, you can access a service known as WordPress that allows ordinary people without much programming experience to create some professional-looking web sites. It does so using templates, and you will find that you can toy with them until you find the precise style that you are looking for. As a professional blogger, I have found that most people tend to use WordPress to set up blogging sites. It is very easy to create new postings, and you can set it up to allow outsiders to post. It is also easy to add pictures, links, and other necessary features to a posting.

While I am on the subject of blogging, your web site is also a place where you can start your blog. Blogging is a good way of showing people that you are working on your application. The format of blogging is often a devil-may-care style of writing, so Figure 3-6 might be a typical blogging entry.

Developer Tools and GUIs

I've been considering doing my Application with some other development tools besides the traditional Eclipse IDE. I'm going to have to do a little more research in this, though. What I am hoping is that it will be easy to make my Application available for other platforms, but only if we start that out from the beginning.

As for the User Interface, I am considering using some type of GUI Prototyping in order to figure out what it will look like. I will probably download several, and probably go with the one that is the easiest to work with.

With any luck, I'll come up with something, and have something that someone else can see, and know exactly what I am trying to do.

Figure 3-6. What a blog entry from an application's web site might look like. This one was made with WordPress.

Note that the way the post is written conveys that you are a human being as well as a developer. It shows that you are trying to make something work, not just trying to do something that will make money. You might also notice that there are things that you don't want to put in a blog, even though they are true. You might not want to state that a certain company that you are working with is giving you a hard time, as this hurts the reputation of the company. Also, you might want to avoid NSFW (not suitable for work) language.

Blogging is also an excellent way of unofficially tracking your progress. Note my use of the word "unofficially." You will definitely want to track the progress of your application's building, launch, and all marketing before and after. There are several reasons for this, and many of them have to do with keeping adequate records for tax time or an IRS audit.

By the way, if you are not an official business, then you should be. If you are in the United States, then you will have to apply with your state's Secretary of State. This can be easily done online, and if you perform a search for your state's Secretary of State, then you should find the documents that need to be filled out to declare yourself a business. I applied as a content writer, but you can apply as a developer or some similar business. The point is that you want the official license, which will cost you a little bit of money depending on what state you reside in. You should take care of this before you get out your first application to the market, as you might want to list a business for the application developer on the Android Market.

Your web site is one of the best tools for creating a following. You'll definitely want to include a community forum on your site. It is easy to create one of these in order to generate some chatter when it comes to your application, even before it launches. I'll go into greater detail on that later in this book, including a discussion on press releases and other communication to the public.

Notice that most web sites have a FAQ. Granted, you won't have any customers before you officially launch your application, but perhaps you can arrange some answers to the question of when your application will be launching. You might also want to answer questions on other platforms that it will be available for, projected cost, and other issues that a potential user would want to know about. Also, you could make a blog entry explaining to readers that you are working on an FAQ section, and you want to see questions for it. You will hear me repeat this several times within this book, but take advantage of any stage that you can stand on. In the case of your application, your web site is the center stage, so put your best work there.

Summary

Think of your application as a performance in and of itself. Just like any performance of a play or movie, there is always some theme that it carries with it. In the case of your application, your theme is the main idea that will form the culture around your application.

Try to see the bigger picture of your application in order to see who is going to be your following and what your application will give them. Once you have determined that, you can figure out the style of your application, and this will help you form your icon, logo, UI, and every visual aspect of your application, including the official web site.

In addition to writing your application and finding your target audience, it is also important to establish a culture around your application. The culture is what your audience believes your application will do for them, and its members will help spread the word on your product. As a developer, it is your responsibility to define your culture, and to create a unique style for your application. This style will be apparent in your icon, logo, UI, and web site.

Developing your application as a culture is important as it involves the audience in the creative process of the application as well as its use. Hearing your audience's feedback will be valuable in future versions of the application, and will ensure that it has a long life on mobile platforms and beyond.

CHAPTER 4

Marketing Your Android Application

We have covered a lot in the last few chapters. At this point, you should have already downloaded some developer tools and worked with programming in Android to get your application up and running, as discussed in Chapter 1. You should have a good idea of what your application will do, determined your target audience, and answered all the questions I asked in Chapter 2. I also hope that you have determined what type of culture it will bring to the Android Market, as discussed in Chapter 3.

If so, then I'm quite certain that you have learned how difficult programming an application can be. You probably know the frustration of getting your program to run without errors. Even without any errors, the greater frustration comes when you can't get your application to do what you want.

All I can say is that I hope you have some help. While it is true that the world of developing software is made for the do-it-yourself (DIY) guy (or gal), it is a proven fact that working with a team creates less work for each member. The reason why I am saying this is because I am about to put more on your plate as a developer, and you might want to find someone else to handle your marketing plan for your application if you haven't already.

How Did You Hear About Your Android Applications?

I want you to do something for me first. Go ahead and look at the home screen of your Android tablet or smartphone, as shown in Figure 4-1.

Figure 4-1. *The typical look of an Android home screen. Some of these applications are used daily, some not at all.*

I'm sure you will see a collection of many application icons that will fall in one of three classifications:

- *Type 1: Applications that are used daily.* For me, these are Text Messaging, E-mail, Calendar, Firefox, Android Market, QuickOffice, and Angry Birds. Many of these applications I have as the first icons I see when I unlock my screen on my Motorola Droid X.

- *Type 2: Applications that are used every once in a while.* For me, this is YouTube, SoundHound, Barcode Scanner, Dictionary, and others that I want to have ready when the occasional need arises.

- *Type 3: Applications that are used seldom to never.* These are apps that you might have downloaded on a whim, maybe during a fad. These are the programs that you look at and think, "Oh yeah, I remember downloading that," and then say, "Why is this still there?" These are also the first to be deleted whenever you need to clear some more space on your Android device.

If you really want to make money as an Android application developer, you will want to create a type 1 application. These are the types of applications that get the most amounts of downloads, because they are more than just desired: they are needed. This is not to say that you cannot make a living from type 2 or type 3 applications, and the level of need for these applications is different for each individual user.

The main reason why I bring up these three categories for applications is to demonstrate that, unless these applications came with your device, you must have heard of them somehow. Then you thought "I want that," and took the time out of your busy schedule to download them. Since you are going to be asking Android users all around the world to do the same for your application, you had better give them something that is worth it.

Try to think back as to how you discovered a few of each of the three types of applications in the first place. You may have had a friend or family member recommend them. Maybe you even saw them on another Android device and wanted them on your own. Maybe you read about them on a blog. Maybe your friends on Facebook wrote about them on their walls. Maybe one of your coworkers at the office was showing them off around the water cooler or the break room.

In all of these cases, all the people who even just mentioned the application were taking part in marketing an Android application.

Word of Mouth: Your Best and Worst Marketing Strategy

According to the dictionary definition of marketing, it is the process or technique of promoting, selling, and distributing a product or service. In other words, it's about getting the word out for your application so those who desire it can purchase it. As someone who is creating and marketing an application, you have to find that market niche or need, and fill it with something that people either need or want.

Many apps have had great success due to word of mouth, which is the best method of marketing there is. Word of mouth is also the least effective method of marketing, as it is not quite dependable.

In other words, how does word of mouth get started? Some of you who can still remember the 1980s might remember the "you'll tell two friends" Faberge Organics shampoo ad campaign (see Figure 4-2). One such ad features a woman telling the audience, "When I first tried Faberge Organics shampoo . . . it was so good, I told two friends about it . . . and they told two friends . . . and so on, and so on, and so on." All the while, the TV screen fills up with replicas of herself. This old commercial illustrates how word of mouth works. By the time the screen fills up with faces, the product is completely viral.

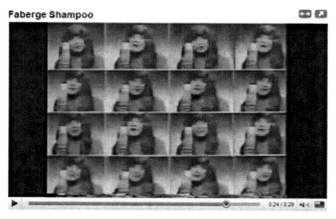

Figure 4-2. *The famous Faberge Organics ad campaign from the 1980s.*

In your case, you are going to be the one who is going to be telling two friends, but you can't possibly expect your two friends to tell two friends, nor for their two friends to tell their two friends. This is why you are going to need a marketing plan, to make certain that you tell more than just two friends. You should tell everyone on social networks.

A marketing plan is more than a method of telling everyone who needs to know so that everyone who will know will spread the word. Marketing is all about making certain that those who want or need the product can obtain it easily.

A lot of word of mouth is due to marketing departments putting words in peoples' mouths. This is why I emphasized that you are selling a culture in Chapter 3. You need a community of followers (for lack of a better word) who are so pleased with your product that they share about your application without even realizing it.

Even though that I am in the tech and gadget blogging world, I can honestly say that the best applications that I have heard about are from my wife. Generally, she will be doing something on her phone, and I will look over on her phone and ask, "What's that?" This is the kind of marketing that you won't find on a marketing report.

Creating a Marketing Plan for Your Android Application

By now, you should definitely have a date set for putting your application on the market. Sure, you might not be ready on your launch date, but it helps to set a deadline, even if it is just an estimate of when programming your application will be complete. There are several things that you can be doing to prepare for the launch date:

- Determine the look of the icon, logo, and UI (see Chapter 3).

- Set up the web site, keeping potential users updated about the status of the app.

- Make a list of the first people in the media that you want to tell about the application.

- Set your application up for social networking on Facebook, Twitter, and others. I'll discuss that in the next few sections.

- Determine how you will do your advertising for additional profits, which we will discuss more in Chapters 5, 6, and 7.

Who Are You Going to Tell About Your Android Application?

The answer to that question is obvious: everyone. Technically, when you put something on the Android Market, you have told everyone. However, the chance of everyone hearing about your application is pretty small, unless it is earth-shattering front-page news. Even if your application really is the most innovative thing to hit the Android Market, this big news can easily be ignored. It helps to have unique words in the application's name and description, as that will target a specific group.

The truth is, we live in a world where headlines change daily and news web sites change faster than that, and there really isn't a pattern as to what is the biggest story. I still can't figure out why we talk about Charlie Sheen, Paris Hilton, or Kim Kardashian. As I said before, word of mouth is a fickle thing. You can try to put out an application that covers current trends, but there is no guarantee that the fad will still be there by the time the application is done.

So, as you write your application, you should be thinking about people in the media that you will want to inform when it is complete. Not only that, but you'll also want to figure out how you are going to tell them. You will want a press release, which I'll cover in Chapter 8 when I discuss your "prerelease buzz."

For now, you should find media outlets such as blogs, journals, and others that would be interested in reporting on an application like yours.

Blogs

Web logging, or blogging, has really grown into a phenomenon in the last decade. It is interesting to see how journalism continues to change thanks to the blogosphere. The digital format of the Internet makes everyone a writer, and with no waiting on the printing press, news is made as quickly as one can write it. Practically everyone who owns a computer has a blog, and there are several that are backed by big media companies who hire out bloggers for paid work.

There are many blogs whose sole purpose in life is reporting on any advancement in tech. As a professional tech blogger, I have reported for a few of them, and I can say that tech blogs are some of the best ways to get the word out on any technological product, including an Android application.

You can run a search on tech and gadget blogs in any search engine, and you will have quite a list. The ones I read daily are some of the bigger ones, such as Gizmodo.com, Engadget.com, and Crave (owned by Cnet.com). These have followings in the millions, where other tech and gadget blogs are in the hundreds of thousands at best.

Tech and gadget writers are always looking for a scoop. I know that it is a lot easier for me to write about something that has been given to me by someone else. This way, the story becomes a report on my experience, and not just a rephrasing of information on a press release. For best results, you will want to send a reviewer a complimentary copy of the application so that he or she can experience it fully.

You should keep in mind that tech is an ever-changing landscape, and there is always something to report on. Sometimes a big tech story (a new Apple product, a new version of Windows) can eclipse other technological news. You should try to get a contact on your tech blog, but don't be surprised if he or she reads you the "I'm too busy act" at first.

When you go to any of these tech blogs, they will usually have a link for contact information (see Figure 4-3). In some cases, they have some place for leaks. You should be able to contact someone at the blog and get your story about your application known. You should probably start a list of the blogs that you will want to contact when your application is ready.

Figure 4-3. *From the Droid Gamers web site. Note that the Contact link in the Other Info section. This is how a lot of blogs can be contacted.*

Keep in mind that a lot of these tech and gadget blogs have a particular focus on what kind of tech they report about. This Droid Gamers screenshot in Figure 4-3 makes it very obvious about what types of applications it reports on. You don't want to be sending them any Android application that isn't a game of some type, as it will be ignored.

Let me give you another example: I used to write for a blog known as image-acquire.com, which specialized in digital cameras, scanners, and photography. If someone were to send me an idea for a story about an application, I would not write about it unless the camera or camcorder on the Android device was somehow related to the application's functionality.

Therefore, you should check out the tech and gadget site that you will want to submit to, to make certain that it has covered Android applications in the past.

I ran a search on "Android app blogs" and found some blogs that specialize in Android applications. These are probably not the only ones, as I am sure that others have sprung up while this book was being printed. These would be a good place to start for spreading the word about your application:

- Android and Me (http://androidandme.com/): This is an Android blog devoted to news, devices, and applications.

- Android Edge (http://androidedge.com/): This is a blog devoted to "all things Android," which includes news, applications, devices, and games.

- Android Guys (www.androidguys.com/): This is an Android web site devoted to many topics, including conferences/events, hot rumors, news, reviews, and discovering apps.

- Android Tapp (www.androidtapp.com/category/apps-blog/): This is a blog with a rating system from 0 to 5, and it would be excellent if your application made the top of the list.

- Androinica (http://androinica.com/): It is, in its own words, "A Google Android blog," and it reviews apps and covers related news.

- Droid Gamers (http://droidgamers.com/): This site is pretty much what the name implies. Its business card states that it is "the only site dedicated to Android games and gaming." I'm not certain whether that has changed, but if you have a gaming application, then I would highly suggest contacting them.

- Droid Life (www.droid-life.com/): This is a Droid community blog; it reports on general news, reviews phones, and features applications.

- Phandroid (http://phandroid.com/): Here is another blog for Android phone fans, and it includes daily posts about applications and other Android-related news.

- Planet Android (www.planetandroid.com/): This is an interesting blog that is devoted to devices, news, and developers of Android.

Printed Journals

Whoever said that print is dead was quite premature, considering the amount of newspapers and magazines that are still in print. We are a long way from an all-digital media society, and you should take note of the local and national printed journals that cover stories about digital technology.

I live in a small town myself, and if I was in need of some press for my application, I would find out if the town paper had some sort of tech section or even one on applications. I would then check the masthead to see who the editor of the tech section is. If it is not listed, then I would make a call to the editor and see if he or she would be interested in doing a report on the latest application for Android . . . mine!

The same rule applies for going to papers or magazines with a much larger circulation. However, you don't want to be limited to talking to the guy in charge of the tech section. For example, if you have an application that is made for the stock market, don't you think the editor of the Investment section of a newspaper would be interested in this? As long as it is useful, the answer is yes, by the way. You should check the Sunday or weekend versions of national newspapers to see what sections your applications could apply to. You should also do the same for any magazines that might be interested in an application like yours.

Social Networking

Where would we be without social networking? Probably with a lot more free time, but a little less connected. I'm pretty certain that I would have fewer "friends," but the very word itself has changed meaning. I can't think of any other place but Facebook where I can see pictures of my friends' vacations, whether I want to or not. It seems like everyone and their dog leaves 140-character comments on Twitter, so it would be wise to develop a group for your social presence.

Facebook

I am just going to assume that you are on Facebook. However, if you are one of those that have never bothered to start social networking, this would be an excellent time to start. Go ahead and get started on www.facebook.com/.

You should take time to set up a group on Facebook that is all about your application or the company that makes your application.

For Facebook, it isn't difficult:

1. Log into your Facebook account. Simply go into the program, and in the left sidebar click Create Group (Figure 4-4).

2. Select a name for your group, definitely something that matches the name of your application.

3. Select an icon for your group.

4. In the Members section, select the friends you want to add to the group.

5. When you get to the Privacy section, you should select Open. You should probably allow anyone to see what is on the group, who is in it, and what members post. Closed groups allow only members to see the posts and what members post.

Figure 4-4. Creating a group on Facebook

You can also build your own Facebook page just by going to www.facebook.com/pages/create.php. Once you log in, you should see a screen like in Figure 4-5.

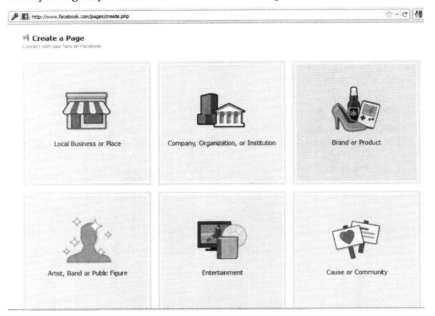

Figure 4-5. *How to create your own page on Facebook*

You can choose from any category provided here, but you have to choose a category and name. You will see a window appear that looks like Figure 4-6.

Figure 4-6. *When you select a box on the Create a Page screen, you will see something like this, unless you select Local Business.*

I selected Brand or Product, but the closest thing to a category for an application that I could find was Software. From there, there are three more steps:

6. *Profile Photo*: I suppose that you could use an image of your or company, but perhaps you have some promotional image, icon, or screenshot that you can use. You have the option of skipping this section for now by clicking the Skip button. See Figure 4-7.

Figure 4-7. *Step 1 of creating a Facebook page for your application and/or business*

7. *Get Fans*: From here, you can set up friends from the get-go to be fans of your new Facebook page. You can also share your page and import your contact list, and send your contacts a message. You can share this page on your wall, and even "Like" your page. See Figure 4-8.

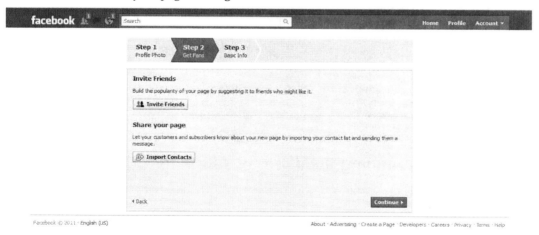

Figure 4-8. *Step 2 of creating a Facebook page for your application and/or business*

8. *Basic Info.* On this screen (see Figure 4-9), you can include the URL for your web site and some information about your page (in 255 characters or less).

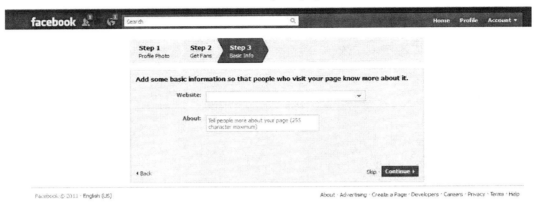

Figure 4-9. *Step 3 of creating a Facebook page for your application and/or business*

Twitter

As for Twitter, it is quite simple to develop a new identity there. Once again, I am going to assume that you already have a Twitter account, but if you don't, you shouldn't feel too out of the loop. Go ahead and go to http://twitter.com/.

Twitter is all about "tweeting"—posting about what you are doing right now in 140 characters or less. You should probably have a username that is similar to the name of your application or your development company, so you should set up an account for it with that name. From there, you can start posting about the progress of your application.

Other Social Networks

I'll talk more about spreading the word on a social network in Chapter 8, but you should probably consider other social networks as well. There are social networks for all kinds of interests. One of them is LinkedIn, the world's largest professional social network.

LinkedIn is a place where you can post your resume, and a terrific place to make business contacts. As a professional blogger, I have found that practically every PR person, company representative, and developer is on LinkedIn. If you haven't done so already, you need to get as many people as you can on your LinkedIn profile.

Other Methods of Spreading the Word for Your Application

Ideally, you want your application to gain so much of a following that the minority sways the majority. Even with articles from blogs and printed journals, and with a social networking presence, there is really nothing you can do to guarantee that your application will go viral. But there are things that you can do to help it along.

SEO Tactics

In Chapter 2, I discussed how to properly name your application, and how to look for possible competition. When you were looking for competitors, you probably figured out that searching for an application like yours was all about finding the right words.

The science of improving the visibility of your product on search engines is known as *search engine optimization (SEO)*. You want your product to show up first on a Google or Android Market search for it, and you can increase the likelihood that it will by making certain that a specific combination of words are used.

Let's say you go through the process and you find the words that you will need. You should definitely go to your web site and incorporate these words as much as you can, but don't over do it. I have seen a lot of interesting sites that have a repetition of certain combinations of words, and this is just so someone who is searching for those words will find the site. It makes the site rather humorous to read in some cases. Proper writing of your content will ensure that it sounds natural, but still have enough keywords thrown in to gain web and application market presence.

Public Relations

As a professional blogger for tech and gadget sites, I often get emails from public relations (PR) companies informing me that they have the latest gadget or application. I imagine that many bloggers get emails like these, and I am certain that the company that made the product hired a PR firm to get the word out about their device.

Hiring a PR firm could save you some time when it comes to getting the word out about your application, as their teams have prepared lists of people that they contact when representing a product. Now, you could develop an entire list of media contacts yourself, and perhaps save some money. That, or just budget out the money to hire the PR firm yourself.

Here are some PR companies that work with developers that want to market their applications:

- *Appular (http://appular.com)*: This company states, "we share your vision of putting high-quality mobile products directly into the hands of users." It has services for marketing, PR, media buying, consulting, and social media.

- *Max Borges Agency (http://maxborgesagency.com/)*: As someone who has been reporting on tech and gadgets for a while, I can say that the PR people at Max Borges do quite a good job getting the word out about the latest technology to people of the press.

- *Westwind Communications (www.iphoneapppublicity.com)*: I realize that the URL of this company says "iPhone," but this company also promotes Android applications.

Sales Goals

Now that you have a marketing plan, you will know what you will do to market your application when the time is right. You should also make a sales goal chart to plan out how your money will be spent. You might have the money to market your application put aside, or you might have investors who are footing the bill. Either way, you are going to need to keep track of the expenses, and part of making sure that you can at least break even is to see where the money is going to go.

Eventually, you are going to have to come up with a number for what you expect to make. Granted, it's always good you make more than you expect, but keep in mind that your numbers might be slightly less than you expect. There are many factors to consider, such as paying Google, who takes 30 percent of sales.

Part of calculating this amount depends on how many downloads you want per day. If you set your goal high, then should try to get a lot of publicity in order to make that goal. You could hire a PR firm to do this for you, provided you have the budget.

A great part of setting sales goals is figuring a price for your app. Considering that most applications are at the $0.99 to $2.99 price point, you had better be offering something completely mind-blowing if you go higher. This is where you have to ask yourself, "Can you afford to offer a lower price?" In case you're launching your app for free at first, I discuss other ways to make money in later chapters, including offering a "Lite" version of your application.

You may have a case where you have a completely unique application; then you definitely have a leg up on your competition (because there isn't any). Or, as I have said in previous chapters, you might be the type who is offering something better than your competitors. Just think how cool it would be if you were offering it for a cheaper price too!

Let me speak to those developers who are going to be sending out multiple applications into the marketplace. As someone who has done a lot of business on eBay, I always have items that I know will win an auction at a high price, and those that probably won't sell unless they are priced cheap.

I guarantee that you will never enter into the Android Market with a handful of gems. Chances are, you will have a few diamonds that make you a lot of profits, some rare stones that give you a worthwhile secondary income, some colored stones that will make enough profits to justify staying in business, and a handful of worthless rocks that you are going to have to either abandon or do some serious work on. Similarly, marketing people have four categories: stars, cash cows, problem children, and dogs.

In other words, not every application you develop will succeed. Marketing will help, but the worst application cannot be saved by the best marketing.

Scheduling Your Launch

If you haven't already done so, you should write up a list of things that need to be done before your application launches, as well as the money that has to be spent to make them happen. A lot of these things will take time, and a lot of these things have to be happening all at once. As a simple example, if you have a plan to get fliers out, you should keep in mind the time it will take to make and print them.

Summary

In addition to the work that goes into making an Android application, there is a lot of work that goes into making a marketing plan. You want to make certain that you are addressing these particular issues while you are working on your Android application; don't wait until the launch date.

I'm certain that you have learned by now how much of a juggling act developing is. You may want to be in front of your computer, working with developer tools, but there is much more to do, including writing content for your web site, obtaining licenses, and other things that will pull you away from writing your application.

If you are programming your application and you get frustrated, take a break and do a search for blogs that might be interested in your application. Or go to Twitter and Facebook, and set up what you will need to give your application some presence in the world of social media.

Think of making an application as a plate-spinning act. The work of programming an app is the most important plate to keep in motion, but you should occasionally spin the plates of media contacts, social networking, and web page updates, among others. It can be a daunting task, so try to set a reasonable goal of when tasks will be completed, as well as your proposed launch date.

CHAPTER 5

How to Promote Android Applications Within Android Applications

Now that you have a plan for marketing your Android applications, you should start thinking about promoting your applications within an application itself.

What I am talking about are ways that you can get more people to notice your application via users who are already using it. Remember what I said in Chapter 3 about how you are selling a culture? Your application users are going to be the best force for getting more users. Although you cannot control how many users your application will have, you can create a first-rate application for your audience.

Speaking of rate, you probably have noticed when perusing the Android Market that all applications have a rating of one to five stars along with their description. The Android Market takes all the reviews and averages them out. I'm not really certain if any application has achieved a continual perfect five-star rating, but as you can imagine, the ones that are close to that rating of perfection are promoted more, as they are at the top of the search list. This leads to more sales.

Since you will need some fresh reviews for your application, you might want to set up your application so it asks users for their personal review.

Setting Up Your Application for Reviews

One of the easiest ways to set up your application for review by users is to simply put a Button on the app's start screen that will send users to the Android Market. This is not the only way, and you can go online to find other code that will achieve the same effect.

I delve into this more in Chapter 12, but it is pretty simple to make a Button in Eclipse. Go ahead and open your application, and go to the main.xml page. Somewhere within your layout (also explained in Chapter 12) you can type in the code for your Button. You can also go into the graphical layout, found in the bottom-left corner of the editor window, and drag and drop a Button on your screen.

Here is an example of some code for a Button; yours may look different depending on its placement on the screen. It should have at least some of these elements.

```
<Button android:layout_height="wrap_content"
android:id="@+id/btnReview"
android:text="Review this application on the Android Market!"
android:layout_width="wrap_content" android:layout_above="@+id/btnGiving"
</Button>
```

I gave it the ID of btnReview specifically so I, the developer, will know what the Button will do when it is clicked. I also assigned it the text "Review this application on the Android Market!" so the user will know what the Button will do when it is clicked.

I am going to need a new screen to open for viewing the Android Market, so I am going to have to create an XML file in the layout file. I'll go into greater detail with illustrations in Chapter 12, but here is what needs to be done:

1. Right-click the res/layout folder in Package Explorer, select New, and then select Other.

2. You will see a new window created. Select the file marked XML and then the XML file marked with an *X* before it.

3. Click Next.

4. Name your XML file something that you will remember later, such as website.xml.

5. Click Finish.

6. Open the new XML file and delete whatever code is there. You can then enter in this code:

```
<?xml version="1.0" encoding="utf-8"?>
<WebView xmlns:android="http://schemas.android.com/apk/res/android"
    android:id="@+id/webview"
    android:layout_width="fill_parent"
    android:layout_height="fill_parent"
/>
```

This will ensure a web browser view of whatever you like, which you will determine in a new activity in the src file. Here is how you can do that.

7. In the src file, right-click the package folder of your application. Select New, and then select Class.

8. Fill in the appropriate information in the window that opens up, and name it something like ReviewActivity.java so you will remember it later.

9. In the Superclass section, name it android.app.Activity.

10. Click Finish.

11. Open the ReviewActivity.java file and copy this code:

```
package New.Project;

import android.app.Activity;
import android.os.Bundle;
import android.view.KeyEvent;
import android.view.View;
import android.view.View.OnClickListener;
import android.webkit.WebView;
import android.webkit.WebViewClient;

public class WebsiteActivity extends Activity implements OnClickListener  {
```

```
        WebView webView;

    @Override
    public void onCreate(Bundle savedInstanceState) {
        super.onCreate(savedInstanceState);
        setContentView(R.layout.website);

        webView = (WebView) findViewById(R.id.webview);
        webView.getSettings().setJavaScriptEnabled(true);
        webView.loadUrl("Your application on the Android Market");

        webView.setWebViewClient(new HelloWebViewClient());
    }

    public void onClick(View v) {
    }

    private class HelloWebViewClient extends WebViewClient {
        @Override
        public boolean shouldOverrideUrlLoading(WebView view, String url) {
            view.loadUrl(url);
            return true;
        }
    }

    public boolean onKeyDown(int keyCode, KeyEvent event) {
        if ((keyCode == KeyEvent.KEYCODE_BACK) && webView.canGoBack()) {
            webView.goBack();
            return true;
        }
        return super.onKeyDown(keyCode, event);
    }
}
```

On the line marked webView.loadUrl("Your application on the Android Market"), what will be in quotes is the URL of your application on the Android Market. You will need to copy and paste the specific URL for your application from the Android Market between the quotes.

You will need to go to your application's activity page in src and alter the activity so your Review Button will work. You can do that with some lines of code. You will want to change the code so it implements OnClickListener. You will also want to add some import statements like these:

```
import android.widget.Button;
import android.view.View;
import android.view.View.OnClickListener;
```

Here is the code that you need for the Button:

```
Button btnReview = (Button)findViewById(R.id.btnReview);
        btnReview.setOnClickListener(this);
```

You will also need to set the Button up with this:

```
public void onClick(View v) {
        Button Button = (Button)v;
```

```
intent = new Intent(v.getContext(), ["Your Activity here].class);
            startActivity(intent);
```

Only one more thing remains: changing the Android manifest.
Right before the last section of

```
</application>
</manifest> :
```

insert this piece of code to set up the web site:

```
<activity android:name=".ReviewActivity" android:label="Review this application"
android:theme="@android:style/Theme.NoTitleBar">
            <intent-filter android:label="Review this application">
            <category android:name="android.intent.category.DEFAULT" />
        </intent-filter>
    </activity>
```

This lets the manifest know that there will be other activities going on that will cause the changing of screens.

You also have to put code in the Android manifest that lets it know that your application is going to the Internet. This can be done like this example at the first part of the code:

```
<?xml version="1.0" encoding="utf-8"?>
<manifest xmlns:android="http://schemas.android.com/apk/res/android"
    package="New.Project"
    android:versionCode="1"
    android:versionName="1.0">
    <uses-sdk android:minSdkVersion="8" />
    <uses-permission android:name="android.permission.INTERNET"/>
```

Go ahead and run your program, and you should see something like Figure 5-1 when you click "Review the application."

Figure 5-1. *If the code is set up right, users can review your application from the application itself just by clicking a button.*

Timing Is Everything

Note that giving the user a chance to review your application at the very beginning is convenient; however, it could become inconvenient. There are some people who will never leave a review, and of these people, there is a certain percentage who will stop using your application because they are sick of being asked to review it.

Do you really want your user to say, "I'm sick of you asking me to review this application all the time! You want a review? I'll give you a review!" I'm sure you can figure out what type of rating an agitated user will give.

In other words, you might want to stop asking for a review when you feel that you have asked enough. After that, allow the users access to your application without feeling that they have to do more. This is why the preceding code has a space for a time limit.

Yes, when it comes to marketing, it is all about reaching the right people at the right time. You might also consider other strategies of getting people to review your application, like when they are in the best possible mood or when they have reached a certain milestone in the application.

For example, if you have a gaming application, and your user/player has just reached a high score, isn't this a great time for them to review your application?

Say you have a productivity application, and the user has just completed something interesting on it. Say he or she just edited their first document. Take advantage of their sense of accomplishment and ask the user to rate your application then.

As you might have guessed, you'll probably have to do a lot of tweaking of the code to get it the way that you want it at the opportune time. However, getting a positive review when a user is in a good mood is worth the extra work.

Sharing an Application on a Social Network

A lot of gaming applications make it quite easy for the user/player to post their high scores to Twitter and Facebook. There are reasons for this that go beyond the user's urge to brag, as this is a very effective marketing technique (see Figure 5-2).

Figure 5-2. *At the end of Doodle Jump, the user/player has the option of sharing his or her score on Facebook. Is this feature for the user, the developer, or both?*

By simply agreeing to post their high score on a social networking site, the user is letting all their Facebook friends and Twitter followers know that they have been playing a game, and that game is your application. As a result, word of mouth will spread about your application, and more people will download it.

Both Twitter and Facebook have sites devoted to developers that will help them program their applications for social networking. The one for Twitter is https://dev.twitter.com/ and the Facebook one is http://developers.facebook.com/.

Another simple way to create a link to Twitter or Facebook from within the application is to use the procedures that I instructed for getting a review. What you need to do is just alter the code for the line webView.loadUrl("Your application on the Android Market") to read webView.loadUrl("http://www.facebook.com") or webView.loadUrl("http://www.twitter.com").

You should change the Buttons' android:id to something like btnFacebook and btnTwitter, and you should change the text to something like "Share on Facebook" and "Share on Twitter." You could use words on the Buttons to do that, but I would highly suggest creating an ImageButton. An ImageButton allows the developer to create a bitmap image that the user can click to get a result.

An ImageButton is created like a Button is in the main.xml file. The difference is that you want to specify a source for the image that you are using. Here is some sample code that you can use and tamper with:

```
<ImageButton android:id="@+id/Facebookbtn"
                android:layout_width="wrap_content"
                android:layout_height="wrap_content"
                android:src="@drawable/facebook_logo">
</ImageButton>
```

In case you are wondering what is meant by facebook_logo, this is what I recommend for any Button that links to the social network. I mentioned in earlier chapters that images create more recognition than words. So if you want users to share about your application on Twitter and Facebook, then you had better make it easy for them by putting the logo of a social network right on the application.

In Chapter 12, I discuss how to upload an icon and background to your application. You can read the particulars about it there, but I will let you know that it is all about moving the image for your ImageButton into the res/drawable file. You should be able to find an image of the Facebook and Twitter logo online, and you will want to be certain that it is a good length and width before you upload it to the drawable file. You will want to make certain that the name of the image file is the same, like facebook_logo in this example.

There are other options for sharing on social networks as well. Figure 5-3 is a screenshot of a game called Ninjump, from Backflip Studios. Like most games, it prompts you to send your high score to Twitter, Facebook, and another option opens up quite a list.

Figure 5-3. *What you will see at the end of Ninjump, when a high score is achieved.*

If you click the envelope in Figure 5-3, it will open up a whole list of media that you can use to share your high score on Ninjump. On this list is Bluetooth, Doc, Email, Evernote, Facebook, Gmail, Goggles, Online Album, Photo Sharing, Picasa, Print to Retail, Text Messaging, Twitter, and Yahoo Mail. In all honesty, I don't see a reason to have so many ways of sharing, but they are all there.

In the same manner, you can program your application so it will create a list of ways that make it easy for the user to share about your application. As long as you send items to an intent, it can handle any list of programs.

Cross-Promotion: One Application Sells Another

I'm going to assume that you want to have great success as a developer, so you will be developing more than just one best-selling application. This next method of marketing is cross-promotion, and it is essentially giving the user the opportunity to acquire another application of yours by offering him or her a selection of other applications.

Earlier I discussed how you can create a window that will allow a user to easily rate your application. You can also arrange it so you can start your application with a quick ad showing some more of your applications. Figure 5-4 shows an example from Tic-Tac-Toe Free from Optime. On the first menu, you are offered a choice of "more games."

Figure 5-4. *Optime believes that its users want to play more than just Tic-Tac-Toe, which is why it offers them the chance to get more games on its startup menu.*

When "more games" is selected, you can see an example of cross-promotion below with a screen that offers other applications. Touching one will send the Android user on a trip to the market, where the application of choice can be downloaded. You should note that Optime appears above each selection like a banner, which promotes the developer even more.

This comes in handy when you are offering a free version of your application, as the opening screen can offer a premium (or paid) version of your application for your users to purchase right then and there. I will have more to say on that subject in the next chapter. I will also cover Admob, which allows you to run *house ads*, which are ads for your own applications. It is also possible to run only your own house ads, but of course you won't get any compensation if users click them.

If you use cross-promotion, you should definitely consider putting applications together that are in the same category. However, you should also think about the user's needs—ask yourself if the user would be open to buying something similar to your application, and then place it on your personal application market.

For example, when I worked in retail, I was encouraged to do cross-merchandising. It worked by putting two similar items on a display together. So, if you have a fishing pole on sale, it makes sense to add a tackle box, even if the latter is not on sale. The customer might only be interested in a just a fishing pole or just a tackle box, but both work well together. In the end, it is just more convenient for shoppers to buy their things in the same area.

Try to market your applications with the idea of, "If you like *this* application, then you'll like *that* one." Back to the example of Optime, note that it offers simple puzzle-like games like Tic-Tac-Toe and Checkers. If the company has action-oriented, racing, or sports games, it doesn't feel the need to offer them here.

In the same way, you want to put applications of the same category together on the splash screen. Granted, this sort of blocks the user from getting where he or she wants to go (the actual application itself), but studies have shown that this will sell more applications.

If you don't have enough applications to make your own market, you can work with other developers to put your applications on their sites. You could even work with these developers to put their personal application markets on your site! You will definitely need to develop some sort of deal with the other business there and put applications together that go together. Think of it as a symbiotic relationship among Android developers.

Social Gaming Platforms

I have an application on my Droid X that my son just loves, called Kongregate Arcade (Figure 5-5). This application is actually several games, and each of them could easily be an application of its own. I am pretty amazed at what my son can find there sometimes, and yet this is just one of several third-party social gaming platforms available on the Android Market.

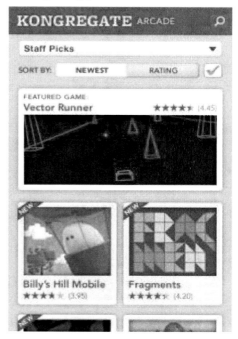

Figure 5-5. The home screen for Kongregate Arcade. It isn't just one gaming application, but many. If you have a gaming application, it might be wise to join a social gaming platform like this.

The format of Kongregate is like the Market itself. The user can choose from a variety of games by category, and then download them to their Android device quite quickly. One that I downloaded even used some cross-promotion at the very beginning, when I selected "more games."

Many of these social gaming platforms have various game services available, including multiplayer games, leaderboards, chat, and achievements. These provide easy ways to get people to talk about your gaming applications.

Summary

One of the best ways to market your application is to get users to do some of the work for you. You can set up your application to allow users to review it the moment it starts. With a bit of code, your application can access Twitter, Facebook, and other places to spread word of mouth about your application.

If you are considering entering the market with more than one application, you will want to figure out how to cross-promote your applications so users can see what other applications you have to offer. For those who are into the gaming applications, there are third-party social gaming platforms that allow users to post their games with other games.

CHAPTER 6

Marketing the Free Application

Now that you have determined your culture, created a marketing plan for release, and figured out ways of selling applications within your own application, it is time to discuss a very important aspect of marketing. Chances are, it will be the first thing that Android Market shoppers will look at when they discover your application: the price.

It doesn't take long before you realize that the most common price for a paid application is $0.99. This is not to say that your application has to be that price, but it definitely has to be worth the price to a user. These days, app users are expecting more from their applications for less of a price. Think of all the games that are free or $0.99, when games of lesser quality used to be purchased for the Atari 2600 or Nintendo Entertainment System for $40.00 in the 1980s.

As someone who usually doesn't pay for applications, I can tell you that I am most drawn to applications that are free. If you are a first-time developer, it might be in your best interest to get your first application out into the market for free. Note the emphasis on the word *might*. If you have created an application that you can get to work well, then why shouldn't you be paid for it?

A lot of paid applications have brand-name recognition going for them, as many years and lots of money have been spent developing their culture, as discussed in Chapter 3. New applications to the market, as good as they might be, can be easily ignored by Android users. It can take weeks, months, or even years before you have a dedicated culture who will be willing to pay for the products that you put out.

Your application is something that you can update over time after it is published to the Android Market. (You will quickly discover how buggy applications can be after their launch, and how they need to be updated periodically.)

Think of your first application as a resume for future clients. If you are in a situation where someone needs a developer, you can show them your first application. The quality of that application could lead to you getting hired to create another application for someone else. If people see that your first endeavor was impressive, they'll tend to believe that you can only get better. Once you get several successful applications on the Android Market, companies will feel more confident about hiring you to create their next winning application.

You might be wondering how in the world anyone can afford to give an Android application away for free, especially with all the hard work that goes into creating an application. However, there are several ways that developers make money apart from the initial price that the user pays for the application:

- *Developing a lite version*: This is when you develop an application separate from your paid version. The lite, or free, version has limited features, but the paid version is the complete package. The idea is that users download the free application just to see what it is like. They then enjoy it so much that they purchase the paid version of your application, which can be released sometime after the free version.

- *Apps that are temporarily free:* You can give your app away and then create a paid version later.

- *Ad revenue:* As with web sites, there is some profit to be made from putting ads within your application. This profit can be great or small, as it depends on the amount of views. If you have some free space on your application's screen, you might as well sell it to those who are willing to advertise on it.

- *Affiliate programs:* This is when a participating company offers a commission every time a sale is generated within the application itself. So far, this is not really used as much as it is on iOS, but that may change.

- *In-app sales:* I will inform you how to do this in the next chapter, but it is a way of allowing your users to buy items within your application to make yet even more profits.

Developing a Lite Version of Your Application

The lite-version strategy is like the free samples at the supermarket. If customers like what they taste, then they will hopefully buy the product. The age-old method of the free sample works on the Android Market as well.

This has been working on the desktop and laptop for years, and I'm sure most of you have try-before-you-buy versions of applications on your Android device as well. Of course, the free versions always have fewer features then the ones their companies want you to pay for. They often have the word *lite* or *free* in their names to distinguish themselves from their paid versions. It is one of the most popular marketing techniques for an Android application on the market today.

Sadly, the conversion rate of free to paid versions of applications is quite low. Some say it is as low as 1 percent, which means that you are going to have to give out a lot of free product to make a profit on the 1 in 100 who upgrades to the paid version. This is something to consider in your sales plan, discussed in Chapter 4.

Most developers write and release their paid and full versions in parallel so that they can release both versions on the same day. The advantage of developing these two applications simultaneously is pretty obvious, and you will probably have many users scooping up the free version on the release date, and the few who might be willing to take a chance on purchasing the paid version. Assuming that the free version is good, but not as good as the paid version, some will upgrade.

Free For Now

There is another way to go about free versions. Remember what I was talking about with establishing a culture, in Chapter 3? It might take a while to really build that culture on your web site and social networks. I suppose that if you are a good enough salesperson, you can convince your online followers to go out and purchase that paid version of your application on the day of its release. If you know how to do that, though, you should probably be writing a book yourself.

It is a lot easier to spread a product if it is free. You could announce that the free version has been released, and watch as your culture, as well as others who enjoy picking up free stuff, download it in droves. You then wait for days, weeks, months, or however long you want before you release the paid version.

The advantage to this is that you can listen to feedback that your free application's audience will undoubtedly have. Users will probably put in their reviews, online chats, or tweets that your application doesn't have a certain feature, or could be improved in some other way. You can then show your audience that you are listening, and develop a pro version of your application that will have everything that your users have been wanting.

While your users are still enjoying the free version of your application, put out the word that a paid version is coming. Spread the word with the resources of your web site, blogs, social networks, and press contacts, and make sure you have set a date for when your paid version will hit the Android Market. By the time the paid version is released, you'll have an audience set up for it. You can decide how long you want the waiting period for the paid application to be, and let the hype build up.

This method of marketing is particularly advantageous for situations where you need more time to develop and enhance your application. As a developer, there will be times when you will not be able to get your application to do what it should, and you simply need more time to learn how to make it do what you want it to do. This is especially true of cases where you are really trying to create something original. This way, you can get your bare-bones application out on the market, and then update it while it is there.

So, you can either do same-day release of the paid and free versions, or delay the paid release. In either case, you are technically creating two different programs according to the Android Market. Therefore, implementing changes and updates on one version means that you will need to implement changes on the other, unless you don't want the free version to have some of these updates.

Differences Between Free and Paid Applications

Since it is up to you to create two different versions of your applications, you must decide how much you want to put in the full and lite versions. This can be a very difficult decision to make, as you have to think about what is best for your business and best for your users. You clearly do not want to give too much of your material away with the free version. If you put too many quality features in the free version, you give the user a valid reason for not buying the paid version of your application.

You also don't want to include what are known on iOS as *crippled features*. This is when your free application informs a user that it cannot do something, but the paid version can. It is usually done in the form of a window and a "Buy Now!" prompt. Like I said in Chapter 5, you don't want to annoy a user with too many requests for them to upgrade.

I'll talk more on that later, but let's talk about what your free application needs to have. First of all, it should be as free of bugs as you can make it. You don't want to have a user dismiss the idea of purchasing a paid version of the application because the free one is terrible or lagging. The problem with developing the free application is that the developer has to purposely limit the features. Think of the free version as the appetizer, while the paid version is the full meal.

On a gaming application, deciding on free application content tends to be easier. Every game has levels, so most lite versions of the game just include the first few levels. This works very well for Labyrinth Lite. Labyrinth is an application where the player has to guide a metal marble through a wooden maze that is full of holes. Controls are all done through the accerlerometer as the user tilts and shifts the ball to the end area. If the ball falls into a hole, then the user has to go back to the start.

Labyrinth Lite is a very addictive game, by design. As you can see on the splash page, the full version has over 1,000 levels. The lite version, on the other hand, only has 10.

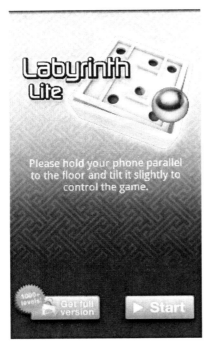

Figure 6-1. Labyrinth Lite is set up from the get-go for the user to get the full version.

As a developer, you have to figure out a good cutting-off point for the free version. For example, if you have a game where the player has to defeat a certain powerful enemy or boss at the end of a level, don't cut off the free version before they face the boss. If you have set up this boss as a powerful challenge and then just end the game there, then a user might not want to play the game anymore because he or she doesn't want the challenge. Instead, cut the free version of the game off after the user defeats the big boss and ends the level. The user then feels a sense of accomplishment, and will download the full version just to get more of this good feeling.

If you are planning this method for a paid gaming application, be sure to cut the user/player off at levels when the game is getting the most addictive. Do not just put in a few levels of the game and expect users to pay for it all. In the full version of your gaming application, give your users more than just all levels of the game. Developers usually like to give their users some interesting bonuses like more in-game supplies or character avatars—anything that makes game play more fun or more interesting.

One thing that I noticed about Labyrinth Lite is that it has the feature of allowing a user to create content. I've tried it out for myself, and the web site makes it easy for any user to create their own maze that is literally full of holes. I could even play on the very maze that I created. In a sense, Labyrinth Lite doesn't just give me ten levels, but infinite.

The user content–creation feature is something that could have been limited to the paid application, but it is handy to have it in the lite version, as most of the 1,000 levels were created by Labyrinth users. It was smart of Illusion Labs to ensure that Labyrinth Lite had this feature, as it has caused the Labyrinth culture to grow, and the application to be more extensive. In the same manner, you don't want to cut off all features on your free version, but keep the ones that can help better market the paid version. Just as the user content–creation feature helps build more Labyrinth culture, your free application needs to have features that help build your culture. More free users lead to more paying users.

As for other types of applications, the developer has to get creative. For example, if you have a note-taking application, you might have to limit the number of lines that it can contain, but not cripple it.

Let me explain that there is a difference between aggressive selling and crippling an application. As mentioned before, the free version is going to have fewer features than the paid one. However, that free version has to be able to stand alone. Any promised feature in the free version has to be delivered, not stopped midway for some annoying reminder that only the paid version can do perform the desired action. In other words, don't have a button on your free version that promises something, but then delivers a "Buy Now!" when pushed.

You should remind the user of the free version of your application that a paid version is readily available, and give him or her access to it. You do not want to overdo this, and you don't want to put excessive dialog windows in the code of the free application that do nothing more than annoy the user. A simple reminder on the home screen is enough, and perhaps a few reminders, but don't remind them every time an intent is invoked. If anything, this makes the user want to buy the paid version even less.

Let's look at another example of an application that has both free and paid versions: Quickoffice (see Figure 6-2). I have a free version that came with my phone that is good for viewing Microsoft Word, Excel, PowerPoint, and Adobe documents. However, if I upgraded to Quickoffice Pro, I could create and edit documents, and access files remotely with the connected file manager. That would certainly increase my productivity on my Droid X, and it is worth the $14.99.

Figure 6-2. With Quickoffice Pro, you can create documents. The free version is just a viewer, which makes the pro version worth its $14.99 price.

Personally, I really like the ability to create and edit documents while I am on the road, even though I can do a lot better work from my laptop. The free version of Quickoffice allows me to create and edit documents in Quickword, provided they stay on the mobile versions. If I want to start taking them off my mobile device and using them, it becomes a real hassle of copying and pasting just to make it work. As far as using Quickword for note taking, though, it is a very good choice.

On the home screen in Figure 6-3 there is a prompt in the lower-left corner inviting users to update their application to the paid $14.99 version. That is really about all that it needs.

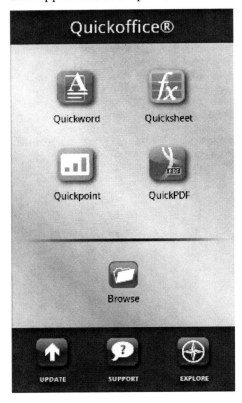

Figure 6-3. The opening screen of the free version of Quickoffice. Note that you can update from here, which may or may not be the only reminder you will need.

If I go into Quickpoint (under the bar graph icon in Figure 6-3), which is essentially a mobile version of Microsoft's PowerPoint, I can only view a PowerPoint document that I have created on my laptop and moved over to my phone. At no point when I click Quickpoint will it open a dialog window that says, "Do you want to create a PowerPoint Document? Please click here to update to Quickoffice Pro." Although it is good to be reminded of that feature, I certainly don't need it all the time. If the free version of Quickoffice had a button that said, "Create New PowerPoint Document," and then gave the prompting to buy the paid version, that would be an example of a crippled feature.

SoundHound, the music audio application, has another way of providing free and paid versions (see Figure 6-4). If you are not familiar with SoundHound, it is a program that can identify a song that is playing—it is one of several applications that can do this. The free version offers the user the chance to look up the lyrics, search on YouTube, and even buy the MP3.

There is also SoundHound ∞ (infinity), which is ad-free and has more features.

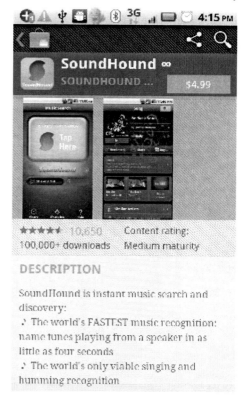

Figure 6-4. A lot of Android users have the free version of SoundHound for identifying songs, but there are more features available on the SoundHound ∞ version.

Yes, removing the ads is usually a paid-app standard, and that is one way of upgrading your free one. However, this leads to the question of when to prompt the user to get the upgrade.

When to Ask Your Users for an Upgrade

Here's an interesting fact that I have heard about lite versions of Android applications. A lot of developers do not put a link to the full version on their lite version. I have heard this from more than one source, and I think it is just plain crazy not to put some sort of link on the free version to buy the full one. That's like a regular store giving away a free bite of their product and not informing people that there was more that the customers could buy.

I can see why most developers don't go out of their way to inform the users of their applications that they can upgrade. For one reason, they probably learned from programming on iOS that the App Store frowns on constant reminders for upgrading. I don't think the Android market has these types of restrictions, but as I have explained before, constant reminders don't always lead to constant buyers. For another reason, doing a search on the Android market for a specific name of an application will usually bring up the lite and full versions.

I say that if you are going to want your users to buy the full version of your application, then you should make it easy on them. Think of what Amazon does with one-click shopping. The easier you make it on the consumer, the more he or she will buy.

Therefore, make it easy for Android users to pay for an application if they want to. Remember what I said in Chapter 5 about how timing is everything when you want your users to review your application or purchase another application? That applies to asking users to buy full versions of your applications.

For example, you can put a quick window on the opening menu that invites the user to purchase the full version, like we saw with Labyrinth Lite. It would also be good to inform the user what he or she will get in the full version at this point. Also, you might arrange it so if a player gets a high score, there will be window that invites the user to buy the full version. To reiterate: Whatever you do, do not make it so you have a crippled feature—for example, if you display the user's high score, and say that he or she can post it in the full version, and then link to the full one. I believe you can do that on Android but not iOS, but maybe you should think more about whether you should (regardless of whether you can).

If you are programming for Android tablets, you might want to take advantage of the large screen to display the full version of your application. The more information you can display about the full version of your application, the more a user will want to buy it.

Advertising on Your Free Application

If the Internet has taught us anything, it is that we can give our product away, and still make some money from advertising. You should be able to make some money on the clickable ads that will appear on your application. It will not be enough to live on, so plan for that.

In the lite version of Angry Birds, there is usually a bar that appears in the corner for ads (see Figure 6-5). I will have to admit that I hit it accidentally, but I've never bought anything on it. This is a prime example of advertising on an application, and you can bet that the paid version is without those ads.

Figure 6-5. *The lite version of Angry Birds. Note the bar for advertising in the corner. Like Rovio's popular mobile game, you can use the space for advertising on your application.*

Hopefully, you have created a plan for how much money will be made, as detailed in Chapter 4. You should figure in that free applications make more money in ad revenue than paid ones. In fact, most paid applications don't have ads. However, in order to make a significant profit from a site with ads, you have to get a lot of downloads.

You can go to several ad network companies that give the user an ad marketplace for developers that want to sell space on their applications. All that is required is just a little bit of code added to your application. Here is a brief list of some of them, and it is by no means exhaustive:

- Adtini
- Jumptap
- Mojiva
- Quattro Wireless
- Traffic Marketplace
- ValueClick Media
- VideoEgg
- Yahoo

Then there are the ad exchanges, who manage to bring together several competing ad companies for business and ensure that there is an ad on display any time your application is open.

AdMob

According to its web site at www.admob.com/, AdMob "provides app developers with a solution to distribute and monetize your apps." It is the world's leading mobile advertising network, it has a huge client list, and its backed by Silicon Valley's top VC firms. It is a significant presence on mobile platforms, and it was acquired by Google in May of 2010 (see Figure 6-6).

Figure 6-6. The home screen for Admob. Not only can Admob service ads for Android applications, but it has a special section called "The Guide to the App Galaxy."

If you already have a Gmail account and you go to Admob's site, it is easy to register. All that is required is to log in with a Gmail account, and you will receive a confirmation e-mail that gives you the following:

- Step-by-step instructions for creating ads and starting your campaign

- Information about tools available for advertisers

- Information about tools for publishers

Also included in the confirmation e-mail is a link to the help center. Granted, this will only help you if you are an advertiser, but even as a developer you should know what happens here.

The advertiser will start a campaign—a way that their ads will be presented on applications. The advertisers enter in a start date, end date, budget, and delivery method. They will then be asked to choose an ad group to meet advertising goals, as well as be given the opportunity to add multiple ad groups. They can then customize what devices that they want the ad on, as well as the countries and operators they want targeted. Advertisers can customize the user demographic, run a text ad or a banner ad unit, and design them as they see fit. The ads will then begin to run, and the advertisers can monitor the campaign's performance.

Okay, that's how it works for advertisers, but let's gets back to you, the developer. For app integration, you will need to have your application finished and published, as discussed in Chapter 9. Follow these steps:

1. Register and/or login at www.admob.com/. If you have a Google account, all you need to do is enter your password.

2. Click the Sites & Apps tabs at the top.

3. Click Add Site/App. You will see a screen like the one in Figure 6-7.

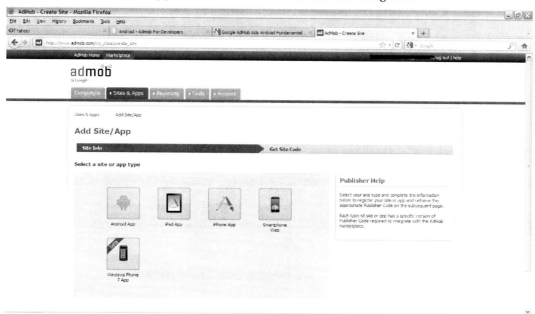

Figure 6-7. *Setting up ads for your application on Admob*

4. Provide the information about the Android application, as shown in Figure 6-8. You will need to use the full application name for App Name. For the Android Package URL, you should go to the Android Market, and copy and paste the URL for your application on the Android Market. Category will be the same, and you can create the description. Click Continue.

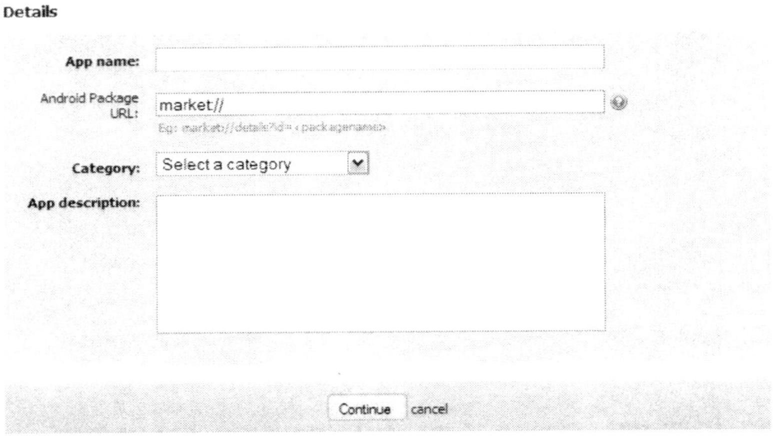

Details

App name:

Android Package URL: market://
Eg: market://details?id= <packagename>

Category: Select a category

App description:

Continue cancel

Figure 6-8. *After you select the type of application, you need to fill out the details.*

5. You will see a screen like in Figure 6-9. Click the Download the SDK button.

Figure 6-9. *What you see after you register your app*

6. Save the Android SDK in a place where you will remember it.

7. Open your application in Eclipse. Right-click your application in Package Explorer. Select New, and then select Folder. You will see a window like in Figure 6-10.

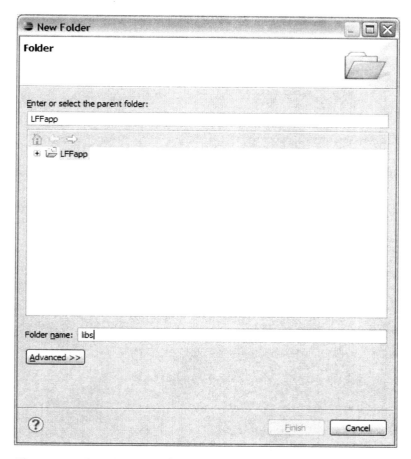

Figure 6-10. Opening a new file on Eclipse

8. For the "Folder name" section, enter **libs**.

9. Go to your file manager, and open up the file where you keep GoogleAdMobAdsSdk. The version you have might be different than the one you have in Figure 6-11.

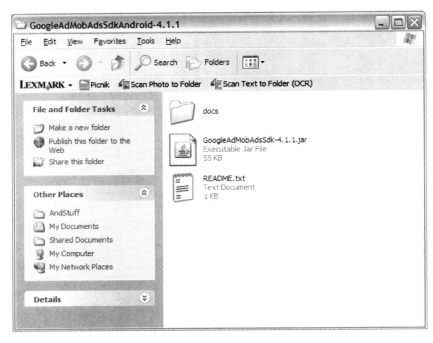

Figure 6-11. *The Google AdMob Sdk folder, ready to be used for ads on your application*

10. Copy whatever version you have of the executable JAR file `GoogleAdMobAdsSdk`, and paste it onto your application's new `libs` file that you just created. You will have to right-click the `libs` file and click Refresh to get it working.

11. Now it is time to get some code in your application.

Go into the `AndroidManifest` file and add the following code right before the last `<application>` and `<manifest>`:

```
<application android:icon="@drawable/icon" android:label="@string/app_name"
            android:debuggable="true">
  <activity android:label="@string/app_name" android:name="BannerExample">
    <intent-filter>
      <action android:name="android.intent.action.MAIN"/>
      <category android:name="android.intent.category.LAUNCHER"/>
    </intent-filter>
  </activity>
  <activity android:name="com.google.ads.AdActivity"
            android:configChanges="keyboard|keyboardHidden|orientation"/>
```

You will have to add this line of code in the manifest as well:

```
<uses-permission android:name="android.permission.ACCESS_NETWORK_STATE"/>
```

You will then need to add this to the main.xml program:

```xml
<?xml version="1.0" encoding="utf-8"?>
<LinearLayout xmlns:android="http://schemas.android.com/apk/res/android"
              xmlns:ads="http://schemas.android.com/apk/lib/com.google.ads"
              android:orientation="vertical"
              android:layout_width="fill_parent"
              android:layout_height="fill_parent">
  <com.google.ads.AdView android:id="@+id/adView"
                          android:layout_width="wrap_content"
                          android:layout_height="wrap_content"
                          ads:adUnitId="MY_AD_UNIT_ID"
                          ads:adSize="BANNER"
                          ads:loadAdOnCreate="true"/>
</LinearLayout>
```

An MY_AD_UNIT_ID is the publisher's ID provided by Admob. You can get that number by logging into your account, clicking Marketplace, selecting Sites & Apps, and clicking Manage Settings in your application.

You should see the ads appear on your application after you have made these updates.

With AdMob comes AdWhirl, which was acquired by AdMob. AdWhirl is an open source ad mediation tool that allows its users to monetize inventory as effectively as possible. Users can allocate inventory to house ads, AdMob ads, and ads from other networks.

Now that you have an idea of how advertising works on Admob for the advertiser and the advertisee, you might want to consider advertising your application with Admob.

Mobclix

In Mobclix's own words, it is "the industry's largest mobile ad exchange network via its sophisticated open marketplace platform and comprehensive account management solution for iPhone application developers, advertisers, ad networks, and agencies." Don't let the word *iPhone* put you off from giving it a try, as it also works on other platforms as well, including Android. Mobclix works with many ad networks, as shown on its web site (see Figure 6-12).

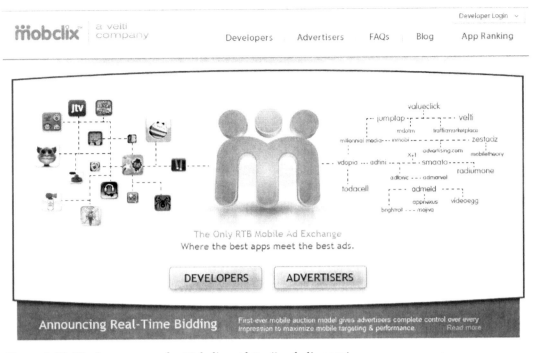

Figure 6-12. The home screen for Mobclix, at http://mobclix.com/

The company boasts the highest *eCPMs*, which are "effective cost per thousand impressions." It translates to the money you will make for every thousand impressions. Mobclix also claims that its monthly infographics can reveal insight on user behavior, so that you can lay out a more thoughtful ad campaign.

Signing up for Mobclix is simple, and it is equally simple to register one's applications. I found that when I signed up, I got a confirmation e-mail that stated that I had to "integrate Mobclix SDK into my app and submit to iTunes." I found that odd, as I want to get started with Android.

You should be able to download the Mobclix Android SDK at http://groups.google.com/group/mobclix-android-sdk?pli=1 for the latest version. The setup is similar to that of Admob. From there, you can use their 100 percent fill rates and analytics to start making money.

Affiliate Programs

The idea of an affiliate program is that a company encourages a developer to send traffic for their retail sales, and a minute commission fee is given out for sales rendered. As someone who has done a little work on the Web, I occasionally receive some profit with affiliate programs like Amazon. They are pretty easy to sign up for and set up, and it is somewhat possible to do this for Android.

I say "somewhat" because I looked around online, and it doesn't appear that Android is set up well for affiliate programs. Like most users, I find that awfully strange. After all, Apple has an iTunes affiliate program that is different depending on your region. In the United States, it is Linkshare.

Unlike iOS, there really isn't much in the way of an affiliate program for Android applications. I'm not certain why Google has not developed a more distinct affiliate program, but I have discovered this: AdMobix has made a recent announcement stating that it is allowing ads to be integrated into an Android application. The company recently released its mobile affiliate marketing platform and SDK for Android. This SDK allows advertisements to be integrated in the application between levels, pageloads, or anywhere on the page.

The AdMobix program has a per-install option that allows developers and advertisers gain additional users and only pay when their product is installed on the customers device, as opposed to the paying per view or click. other options include pay-per-call and pay-per-lead.

You can find out more information about this at AdMobix SDK for Android site at http://blog.adcommunal.net/admobix-sdk-for-android (see Figure 6-13). As of this writing, it is currently in beta.

AdMobix SDK for Android

We are proud to announce that we have just taken AdMobix to the next level!
The brand new AdMobix SDK for Android is now available for beta testers.

It includes:

» A dynamic banner rotator to place in your App

» Configurable refresh intervals

» Interface that allows you to select the campaigns you want to run on your App

Very easy to install: simply include the JAR-File in your Android project, specify your Affiliate ID, place the rotator in your layout and you are all set to monetize your App!

To apply as a beta tester, please email beta@adcommunal.com.

Figure 6-13. A link to sign up for the beta version of AdMobix SDK for Android, an affiliate program for Android applications.

I wouldn't be surprised if Android affiliate markets don't grow more in the near future. If there is one thing that I have learned from business on the Internet, it is that someone usually makes a product if people whine for it enough.

Summary

Android developers can make money from their application if it is available for free to Android users. Giving away a free sample of the application is one of the best ways to entice users to purchase the paid version. It is good for those first-time developers who don't have brand-name recognition, but first-time developers must prove to users that they can create a quality application.

Another way that developers can make profits on their application is through advertising on their application. There are several ad network companies that the user can go through, and also ad exchange companies such as AdMob and Mobclix.

As for affiliates, there aren't really many ways to make a profit on this platform, at least for now. However, this is a growing market, and there should be several ways of making money on affiliate programs for Android applications in the future.

CHAPTER 7

In-App Billing: Putting a Store in Your Application

In Chapter 5, I discussed how an application can have its own store for more applications, and this is one more way that the developer can make profits apart from the initial price and advertising.

Now I am going to suggest ways in which you can make some more money by putting another type of market within your own application. *In-app billing* is only a recent addition to the Android Market, and it can offer the user premium features, unlocked content, and downloads, as well as upgrades and expansion packs. Combined with the free application method mentioned in the previous chapter, your application will follow the "freemium" business model, a method that has been working on many software fronts since the 1980s.

Remember in Chapter 6 how I pointed out that many free apps don't make it easy for the user to obtain the paid version? The same happens for in-app purchases. Many applications do not mention them on the splash screen, but you might want to put them in the description of the application on the market itself. How you want to peddle them within your application is up to you, but like I said in the last chapter (and the one before that), timing is everything. Don't hound the users with constant requests to buy your in-app virtual goods, or you will have fewer users. If you have a home screen menu, it will be very beneficial to make your in-app store one of the selections on it.

Your in-app purchases should be designed to complement the application itself, but users should be able to operate the application without them. Remember the analogy in the last chapter about the free samples at the grocery store? This is the same type of thing, except you get your users to love your application so much that they would be willing to pay for a little (or a lot) of something extra. Pricing is a little tricky in the realm of Android. Apple's in-app sales use a tier system starting at $0.99, which is then converted to local currency for the international market. Android doesn't have any tiers, but there is a currency conversion. You will have to figure out how it will best work for you.

When to Use In-App Billing

In-app billing is also good for games, but unless you can make in-app purchases compatible with your application, it just isn't worth it for some types of applications. I realize that it is tempting to try and make more money, but not all applications require it.

In fact, I'll reiterate a point that I also made in the last chapter about how you want your application to stand alone, without adding crippled features. Don't put in windows that say, "This feature is not available unless you pay for this particular in-app purchase, so buy now." You don't want to offer a free application that will work well only when the user makes some in-app purchase. In other words, don't set your application up so that the user is getting a free application, but is paying for its features.

This is very different for some applications in which the user knows that he or she will need to be paying for something extra upon downloading the application. For example, there are many reader applications, and many of them are free. However, if you want books, then it is implied that the user has to pay for them.

In the case of the Aldiko Book Reader application, it clearly states in the description that the books cost (see Figure 7-1). If you have a player- or reader-type feature where individual e-books or videos cost extra, then you want to put something in your description that states that. I've seen DVD player boxes that show a movie playing from the DVD player, and there is usually some fine print saying, "Television and movie sold separately." You should probably have that fine print, even though it really is obvious.

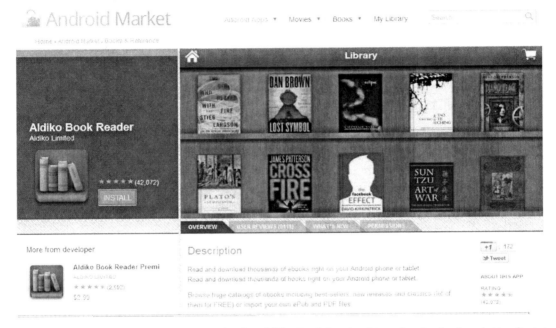

Figure 7-1. *The Android Market entry for the Aldiko Book Reader. Note that in the description it states that not all the books are free.*

I say "probably" because Google Videos, an application designed for viewing movies on Google, does not make any such disclaimer in its description (see Figure 7-2).

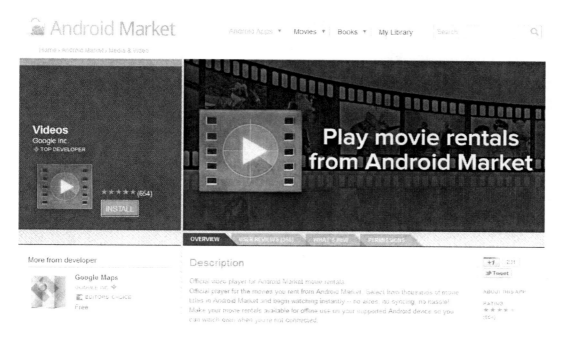

Figure 7-2. Google Videos is free, but movies (which you will have to pay for) are not included.

I'm assuming that a reader or viewer application makes it pretty obvious that you are going to have to pay for something more. If it isn't obvious, then you should use the fine print if you are using a subscription model for your in-app purchases.

Types of In-App Billing

If you try to buy a book on Aldiko Book Reader, you will be taken to the mobile version of feedbooks.com. This book reader application made a deal with Feedbooks so it could have a virtual book store. In the same manner, you can make your own store or try to partner with an online store.

There are many ways to set up in-app billing, but the one that I will talk about most prominently is Google's own in-app billing process. If you use Google's method, Google is going to take 30 percent of whatever you earn from your in-app purchases, which is pretty much what they take from the price of the application. There are others that you can find online that can do the same, with less of a take.

You can sell more on your application than just virtual goods. You can sell physical goods as well if you set up an online market to ship goods to your users. Take a look at part of the opening screen for Rovio's Angry Birds Seasons in Figure 7-3.

Figure 7-3. What you will see on the opening screen for Rovio's Angry Birds Seasons. Touch this and you'll be led to the online store.

You can get more than just Angry Birds plush toys there. You can get flip-flops, backpacks, socks, neckties, and much more. I could probably cover a chapter or two talking about merchandise, as it is a serious money maker for companies like Lucasfilm and Pixar. However, merchandising really isn't worth discussing unless you have a demand for it. In the case of Angry Birds, there are players who want this merchandise, and it is enough for Rovio to justify making it. I'll let you decide whether or not you want to spend the money to create merchandise for your application, but only after you have several million downloads.

For now, you can program your online store to go to any web site, and I have the code for that in Chapter 12. You are going to have to make some sort of partnership with an online store if you want to go that route, or get into the online store business.

In-App Billing for Android

As mentioned in Chapter 6, there is more than one way to make money on an application. One of them is a recent update (just started in March 2011) for Android developers that allows them to sell content from their applications.

Like the in-app purchases introduced on iPhone SDK 3.0, the Android Market in-app billing provides a billing request for specific in-app products, such as virtual goods. The best part is that the application does zero work when handling the financial transactions, as checkout details are handled by the Android Market. This includes requesting and validating in the form of payment and processing, and in-app billing even sends the order number, order time, order date, and price paid to the application.

According to the Android Developers site, some in-app billing implementations use a private remote server in order to deliver content or validate transactions. This remote server can be useful if selling digital content needs to be delivered to a user's device, like photos or media files. It is also helpful for storing the user's transaction history or performing various in-app billing security tasks like signature verification.

Examples of In-App Billing

One example of in-app billing is Comics, by Comixology. Comics is an application that is designed to give Android smartphone and tablet users access to digital versions of their favorite comic books. Downloading the application is free, but some of the comics cost the user. I imagine that Comixology had to make some sort of deal with the comic book companies in order to offer this service, but after those companies receive their share of the profits, Comixology no doubt makes a healthy profit from comic book readers paying for digital comic book content. All that is required of the user is to create an account online, and it syncs up very well (see Figure 7-4).

Figure 7-4. *A screenshot from the store at Comixology, where users can purchase their favorite comic books in digital form*

As you can see, offering digital content for in-app billing is all about giving the customer what they want, and making sure that it lines up with your application. Tap Tap Revenge uses the same kind of marketing in order to sell music tracks. Tap Tap Revenge is a music game where players tap on the screen to the rhythm of their favorite tunes, similar to music games such as Guitar Hero and RockBand. Tap Tap Revenge offers a few songs for free, but if you want more, then you have to pay. I'm sure that the music industry gets their percentage, as well as the developers (see Figure 7-5).

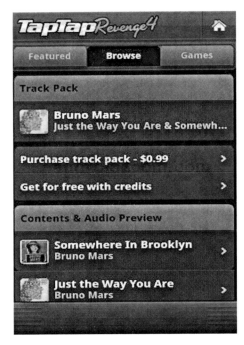

Figure 7-5. Tap Tap Revenge 4 uses in-app billing so the user can purchase more tracks for this music-based game.

Many gaming applications, such as Tap Tap Revenge, have a sort of token economy that allows the user to play the game, and then use points or coins earned within the game to buy bonuses. In Gun Brothers, from Glu Mobile, the user has the opportunity to play a shooting game and earn a lot of points. These points can be used to purchase gun upgrades and so forth. However, if the user wants to take a shortcut and just buy the upgrades, he or she is more than welcome to do that, thanks to in-app billing (see Figure 7-6).

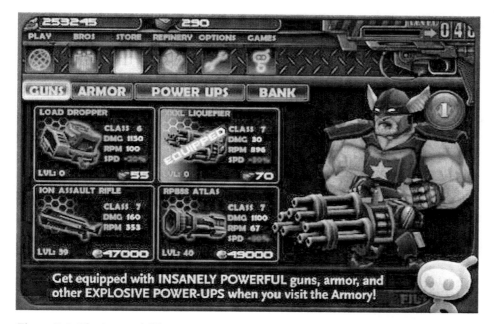

Figure 7-6. *The in-app billing on Gun Brothers allows the user to buy war bucks or coins that can be used for armor, weapons, and power-ups.*

You may be surprised that there is a market for these types of virtual gaming goods, but oddly enough, people actually pay money for game bonuses. This is the beauty of gaming applications: many gamers are willing to lay their money down for things that only exist in a virtual gaming world. That certainly is a positive thing for developers.

Setting Up Your Application for In-App Billing

The Android Developers site can send in-app billing requests and manage in-app billing transactions using the Android Market. It has a sample application that shows the user how to do several in-app billing implementations. It is available now at
`http://developer.android.com/guide/market/billing/billing_integrate.html#billing-download`.

The sample shows you how to handle synchronous responses from the Android Market application, and asynchronous responses (broadcasts intents) from your Android Market application. It also shows you how to use in-app security mechanisms for the integrity of billing responses, and even how to create a UI that allows users to select items for purchase.

This sample includes an application file (`Dungeons.java`), as well as an Android Interface Definition Language (AIDL) file (`IMarketBillingService.aidl`). It also includes several classes that demonstrate in-app billing messaging. It is available on the SDK, and you can get it by simply going to the SDK or Eclipse and opening the Android SDK and AVD Manager. You then just need to select Google Market Billing Package, and then Install, as shown in Figure 7-7.

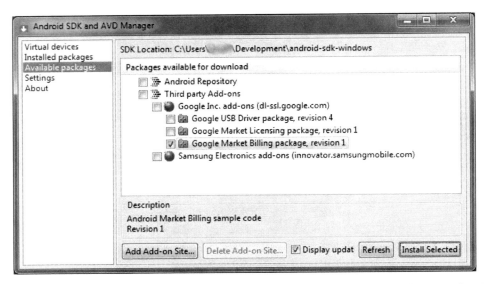

Figure 7-7. Where to find the Google Market billing package in the Android SDK and AVD Manager

The file is located wherever you placed the SDK, in extras/google/market_billing. If you want to see a demonstration, follow the instructions for installing the sample in the next section.

How to Install the Sample

If you want to see a demonstration, then you will need to build and run the sample, configure and build the sample application, update the sample application to the Android Market, set up test accounts, and run the sample application. You also have to add the Android Market public key to the sample application code. Here's how:

1. Log into your Android Market publisher account.

2. Click Edit Profile at the upper left of the page.

3. Scroll down to the Licensing and In-app Billing panel on the Edit Profile page.

4. Copy your public key.

5. Open the src/com/example/dungeons/Security.java file in your editor.

6. Add a public key to this following line of code: String base64EncodedPublicKey = "your public key here";.

7. Save the file.

8. Change the package name of the sample application, since the Android Market does not let you upload applications with package names that contain the text com.example. Its current name is com.example.dungeons.

9. Build the sample application in release mode and sign it.

From there, upload the sample application as a draft to the Android Market publisher site. I discuss the Android Market publisher site in much greater detail in Chapter 9.

You must create a product list for the in-app items available for purchase. To do that, you have to upload the release of the sample application to the Android Market. You don't want to publish it—just leave it as a published draft application. The purpose of it is for a demonstration; it should not be made publicly available yet. You can see a sample of it in Figure 7-8.

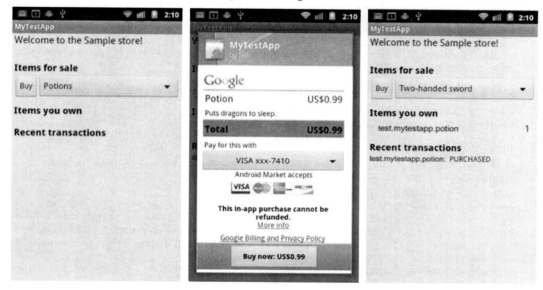

Figure 7-8. *A sample of in-app billing*

Notice that this application creates a product list of sword_001 and potion_001 (very fitting items from a sample file called Dungeons.java). The Android Developers site recommends setting up the purchase type in two ways so you can see how it works. You have to publish the items in your product list, even though you're not publishing the sample application.

The sample application can't be run on the emulator, only on a device. To run it, you have to have at least one test account registered under the Android Market. You will need to verify that the device is running a supported version of the Android Market application or the MyApps application. For example, if your device is running Android 3.0, in-app billing requires version 5.0.12 or higher of the MyApps application; any other version of Android requires version 2.3.4 or higher.

Install the application on the device and make one of your test accounts the primary account on your device. If the primary account isn't a test account, here's how to perform a factory reset:

10. Open Settings on your device.

11. Touch Privacy.

12. Touch "Factory data reset."

13. Touch "Reset phone."

14. Once the phone resets, sign in with your test accounts.

There's nothing left to do but purchase one of the products and see if it works. The test account is billed through Google Checkout, and your Google Checkout Merchant account receives a payout. You'll want to refund purchases made with test accounts, or else these purchases will show up as actual payouts.

Installing In-App Billing Without the Demonstration

The MarketBillingService file has to be added to the project, and the Android build environment creates an interface file (IMarketBillingService.java), and this interface can make billing requests. If you are using Eclipse with its ADT plug-in, just add this file to the src directory, and Eclipse will generate the interface file. It is somewhat easy, and here are the instructions:

1. Create the following director in src: com/android/vending/billing.

2. Copy the IMarketBillingService.aidl file to the sample/src/com/android/vending/billing directory.

3. Build the application.

You should then check the gen folder to see if you can find the generated interface file named IMarketBillingService.

The next steps are updating the application's manifest and adding the com.android.vending.BILLING permission to the AndroidManifest.xml file. You need to declare the BroadcastReceiver that you will use to receive asynchronous response messages, and declare the service that you will use to bind with the IMarketBillingService and send messages to the Android Market. You also need to declare intent filters for the BroadcastReceiver so the Android system knows how to handle the broadcast intents sent from the Android Market application.

Here is the sample code for the in-app billing service:

```
<?xml version="1.0" encoding="utf-8"?>
<manifest xmlns:android="http://schemas.android.com/apk/res/android"
  package="com.example.dungeons"
  android:versionCode="1"
  android:versionName="1.0">

<uses-permission android:name="com.android.vending.BILLING" />

<application android:icon="@drawable/icon" android:label="@string/app_name">
  <activity android:name=".Dungeons" android:label="@string/app_name">
    <intent-filter>
      <action android:name="android.intent.action.MAIN" />
      <category android:name="android.intent.category.LAUNCHER" />
    </intent-filter>
  </activity>

  <service android:name="BillingService" />

  <receiver android:name="BillingReceiver">
    <intent-filter>
      <action android:name="com.android.vending.billing.IN_APP_NOTIFY" />
      <action android:name="com.android.vending.billing.RESPONSE_CODE" />
      <action android:name="com.android.vending.billing.PURCHASE_STATE_CHANGED" />
    </intent-filter>
```

```
  </receiver>

 </application>
</manifest>
```

Next it is time to create a local service in order to facilitate messaging between your application and the Android Market. The service must bind to the MarketBillingService so the application can send billing requests and receive billing responses from the Android Market application.

This is the code for how to use the bindService method:

```
try {
  boolean bindResult = mContext.bindService(
    new Intent("com.android.vending.billing.MarketBillingService.BIND"), this,
    Context.BIND_AUTO_CREATE);
  if (bindResult) {
    Log.i(TAG, "Service bind successful.");
  } else {
    Log.e(TAG, "Could not bind to the MarketBillingService.");
  }
} catch (SecurityException e) {
  Log.e(TAG, "Security exception: " + e);
}
```

You have to reference to the IMarketBillingService interface for making billing requests via IPC method calls. This is the code with the onServiceConnected() callback method:

```
/**
 * The Android system calls this when we are connected to the MarketBillingService.
 */
public void onServiceConnected(ComponentName name, IBinder service) {
  Log.i(TAG, "MarketBillingService connected.");
  mService = IMarketBillingService.Stub.asInterface(service);
}
```

Since you can use the mService reference to invoke the sendBillingRequest() method, use that reference to send billing requests to the MarketBillingService. This is done via IPC method calls, and the single public method sendBillingRequest() takes a single Bundle parameter. This is important so the user can handle five types of transactions:

- *CHECK_BILLING_SUPPORTED*: Verifies that the Android Market application supports in-app billing

- *REQUEST_PURCHASE*: Sends a purchase request for an in-app item

- *GET_PURCHASE_INFORMATION*: Retrieves transaction information for a purchase or refund

- *CONFIRM_NOTIFICATIONS*: Acknowledges that you received the transaction information for a purchase or refund

- *RESTORE_TRANSACTIONS*: Retrieves a user's transaction history for managed purchases

There are details about each one of these at the Android Developers site, at http://developer.android.com/guide/market/billing/billing_integrate.html#billing-service.

Now I will discuss how to create a `BroadcastReceiver` to handle broadcast intents from the Android Market application. The in-app billing application uses broadcast intents in order to send billing responses to your application, but to receive them you need to create a `BroadcastReceiver` that can handle the following intents:

- *com.android.vending.billing.RESPONSE_COD*: Sent after an in-app billing request

- *com.android.vending.billing.IN_APP_NOTIFY*: Indicates a purchase with a changed state, showing a successful, canceled, or refunded purchase

- *com.android.vending.billing.PURCHASE_STATE_CHANGED*: Contains detailed information about one or more transactions

Here is some code to show how to handle the broadcast intents and intent extras within a `BroadcastReceiver`:

```
public class BillingReceiver extends BroadcastReceiver {

  private static final String TAG = "BillingReceiver";

  // Intent actions that we receive in the BillingReceiver from Android Market.
  // These are defined by Android Market and cannot be changed.
  // The sample application defines these in the Consts.java file.
  public static final String ACTION_NOTIFY = "com.android.vending.billing.IN_APP_NOTIFY";
  public static final String ACTION_RESPONSE_CODE =
"com.android.vending.billing.RESPONSE_CODE";
  public static final String ACTION_PURCHASE_STATE_CHANGED =
    "com.android.vending.billing.PURCHASE_STATE_CHANGED";

  // The intent extras that are passed in an intent from Android Market.
  // These are defined by Android Market and cannot be changed.
  // The sample application defines these in the Consts.java file.
  public static final String NOTIFICATION_ID = "notification_id";
  public static final String INAPP_SIGNED_DATA = "inapp_signed_data";
  public static final String INAPP_SIGNATURE = "inapp_signature";
  public static final String INAPP_REQUEST_ID = "request_id";
  public static final String INAPP_RESPONSE_CODE = "response_code";


  @Override
  public void onReceive(Context context, Intent intent) {
    String action = intent.getAction();
    if (ACTION_PURCHASE_STATE_CHANGED.equals(action)) {
      String signedData = intent.getStringExtra(INAPP_SIGNED_DATA);
      String signature = intent.getStringExtra(INAPP_SIGNATURE);
      // Do something with the signedData and the signature.
    } else if (ACTION_NOTIFY.equals(action)) {
      String notifyId = intent.getStringExtra(NOTIFICATION_ID);
      // Do something with the notifyId.
    } else if (ACTION_RESPONSE_CODE.equals(action)) {
      long requestId = intent.getLongExtra(INAPP_REQUEST_ID, -1);
      int responseCodeIndex = intent.getIntExtra(INAPP_RESPONSE_CODE,
        ResponseCode.RESULT_ERROR.ordinal());
```

```
        // Do something with the requestId and the responseCodeIndex.
      } else {
        Log.w(TAG, "unexpected action: " + action);
      }
    }
  }
  // Perform other processing here, such as forwarding intent messages to your local service.
}
```

The BroadcastReceiver must also be able to handle the information received in the broadcast intents, and the BroadcastReceiver accomplishes this by sending information to a local service. The BillingReceiver.java file in the sample application can show you how to do this.

It is now time to create a security-processing component in order to verify the transaction messages that are sent by the Android Market. The Android Market's in-app billing service uses two mechanisms for verifying the transaction information: nonces and signatures. A *nonce* is short for "number used once," and it is a secure number that the application generates and sends with every GET_PURCHASE_INFORMATION and RESTORE_TRANSACTIONS request. The following is some sample code used to generate, manage, and verify nonces:

```
private static final SecureRandom RANDOM = new SecureRandom();
  private static HashSet<Long> sKnownNonces = new HashSet<Long>();

  public static long generateNonce() {
    long nonce = RANDOM.nextLong();
    sKnownNonces.add(nonce);
    return nonce;
  }

  public static void removeNonce(long nonce) {
    sKnownNonces.remove(nonce);
  }

  public static boolean isNonceKnown(long nonce) {
    return sKnownNonces.contains(nonce);
  }
```

As for the application that needs a verification for signatures for every PURCHASE_STATE_CHANGED broadcast intent, the Security.java file shows how to perform this verification. In order to use your Android Market public key to perform the signature verification, here is the procedure:

4. Log into your publisher account.

5. Click "Edit profile" in the upper-left corner of the page, under your name.

6. Scroll down to the Licensing & In-App Billing panel.

7. Copy your public key.

Now, after you are done with that, you can modify the application's code. This means that you need to write code for a storage mechanism for storing the users' purchase information, and create a UI that allows users to select items for purchase.

You should take another step to prevent piracy, and Android encourages developers not to bundle their in-app purchase content into the APK file. It is be better to deliver the content through a real-time service with a remote server, and be certain that the content is encrypted for an SD card.

Figure 7-9 illustrates the architecture.

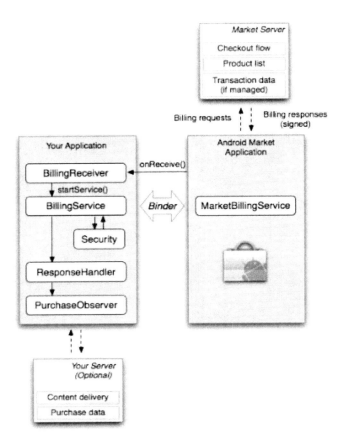

Figure 7-9. The complex architecture of the in-app billing for the Android Market.

Summary

Android developers have been given a chance to receive more profits from their applications with the in-app billing program, as well as online stores that can be accessed within the application itself.

The in-app billing program is perfect for selling virtual goods within the application, and it works well if the developer can create a subscription for their goods. It isn't for every type of application, but it works very well for games.

Setting up an application for in-app billing requires you to head to the Android Developers site, where a sample can be downloaded and tested out before it can be configured. The Android Market handles the security and payments, even though the setup is somewhat complex.

CHAPTER 8

The Prerelease Guide

Remember back in Chapter 4 how I discussed getting started on a marketing plan? Hopefully you have planted the seeds and taken care of the buds, and now it is time to prepare for a harvest.

This chapter is a checklist covering what to do before you set your application free into the Android Market to reap its deserved profits.

Getting the Word Out on the Release Date on Your Official Web Site

By this time, I am going to assume that you have your Android application complete, or you are just putting the finishing touches on it before you will send it to the Android Market. You should definitely have that release date set and be preparing for it, as well as what comes afterward (we'll cover what to do then in Chapter 10).

I am repeating myself when I say that timing is everything, but it can't be said too often that delivering the right message at the right time is really what marketing is all about. By now you may not have all of the application completed, but you should be preparing for the big launch.

The day your application launches is going to be a great time for marketing, as you will actually have the mobile software itself to show off to members of the media. Unless you want to have a period of beta testing, your application should be as perfect as you can get it. Not that there is anything wrong with beta testing (I'll go into more detail about that strategy in the next chapter).

My point is that when that launch date hits, you should have an application worthy of telling the world about. Then you are going to be very busy telling the world, so you should prepare for this roller-coaster ride. You do not want to be trying to juggle too many balls after the application is out there.

You will have to spread the word on every outlet that you can. Start with the web page, put it on the splash page, and post it on the blog, but make certain that it is known and obvious.

Web Site Presence

I already discussed the importance of creating a decent official web site for your application in Chapter 3. Until now, your web site probably doesn't look like much except a place to build your community, a placeholder until you can get your application going. In other words, your web site is nothing more than a shop with "coming soon" signs on it, but now you need to make it obvious that it will be a booming marketplace for your applications.

At this particular time, you should prep your web site so it is set up to sell. This means that you are going to make it clear that you are in the application business. Note several elements in Figure 8-1 that show how to display an application on your official web site.

Figure 8-1. What you will see on the Boolba Labs page (www.boolbalabs.com/). This demonstrates how applications are advertised on the company's official web site.

Notice the application's name (Roll It), and if you go to the site itself, you will see that you can scroll through several gaming applications. You will also notice the company logo, as well as a caption and/or quick-pitch description. The official link to the Android Market is also there, and you should put a Buy button there.

These Market and Buy buttons should be pretty big so it is obvious to the visitor whereto buy the app. You should include a "coming soon" message on it until you finally get your application through the Market.

Boolba Labs' web site shows an image of the application running on an Android phone, but your web site can show a tablet if your application is optimized for that. Showing the application running on a device is a convention for every application's official web site.

If you like, you can put a video on your site, and I will talk about how to make a video of your application later in this chapter. After all, you might as well show the users what your app looks like running on an actual Android device.

You can devote an area to listing features, and you can include benefits and requirements. You can also put up some reviews and testimonials as well. I'm surprised that Boolba didn't include some mechanism that allows the user to easily share on Facebook and Twitter. An example of such a mechanism is shown in Figure 8-2, which displays the web site for Halfbrick's popular gaming application, Fruit Ninja.

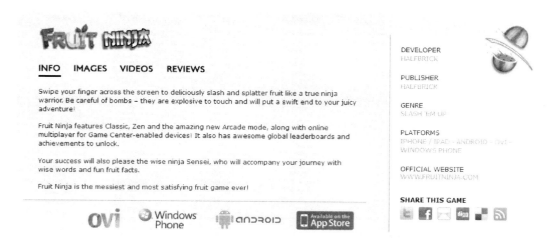

Figure 8-2. Halfbrick's official web site for Fruit Ninja, with links to Twitter, Facebook, and other sites in the lower-right corner, and a link to reviews in the upper-left corner.

Chapter 12 contains is a sample application that shows how to create a button that goes straight to a web site. I highly suggest that you create a button on your application that will link directly to your web site. Follow the example of the code there so your application users can visit your official web site from your application, as well as share on Facebook and Twitter, as discussed in Chapter 5.

Also, you'll want to make a mobile version of your site. There are many ways of doing this, and you can consult one of these many sites to see how:

- Google Conversion Utility (`www.google.com/gwt/n`)

- Mobeezo (`www.mobeezo.com/`)

- Mobify (`http://mobify.com/`)

- mobiSiteGalore (`www.mobisitegalore.com/`)

- Winksite (`http://winksite.com/site/index.cfm`)

- Zinadoo (`www.zinadoo.com/`)

Increasing Your Blogging About Your Application

As your launch date grows closer, you should blog more. The final stages of making an application are often quite interesting, and this would be a good time to start posting about all these final aspects. You should take time to post daily, possibly even twice daily, as your launch date approaches.

If you want to, you can write several blogs at once, and then set it up so that the blog posts go live exactly when you want them to. As someone who has made a living from blogging, this is a trick you can use so you don't have to spend time writing blogs daily during the week. If you are using a WordPress template, it is quite easy to do, as you can schedule a date and time for your blog posts to go live (see Figure 8-3). To do this in WordPress, click Edit in the Publish Immediately section under the Publish column on the right.

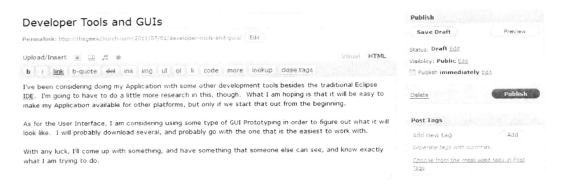

Figure 8-3. *If you are using WordPress to publish your blog on your application's web site, then you can schedule blog posts ahead of time.*

This leads to the question of what you are going to write about. You will need to need to think about your culture to answer that. Think about what your followers on Twitter and Facebook would be interested in hearing about. One a good idea is to talk about the features that you have been promising. Building an application is like making a movie, and I'm sure that you have seen many making-of-a-movie features on DVDs. I must admit that only a few of these are really interesting enough to watch a second time. If you can write about creating your application in a way that is interesting, it will draw readers in.

RSS Feeds and Followers

By now, you hopefully have a lot of subscribers to your blog's RSS feed. Checking to see how many RSS followers you have is an excellent way of discovering your culture, as discussed in Chapter 3. In order to get more followers, you can post links on social media sites such as Twitter and Facebook every time you do a blog post.

But that's if you want to do it the hard way. Instead, I recommend setting up a web service like Posterous, Tumblr, TwitterFeed, or TypePad to automatically put your blog entries on social media sites. This is also possible to set up with blogs like the aforementioned WordPress, as well as Blogger, LiveJournal, and Movable Type.

This is also a time to start looking at the comments on your blog. On WordPress, this is very easy to do from the template, and it may be very useful to hear back from what will hopefully be your application's following before the application is released. From their comments, you might get an idea of what features might be needed before the launch date, or what will need to be added after the application has hit the market. You should also look for concerns in the comments. For example, if you are seeing a lot of comments that the application might be too hard to use, it might be a good idea to take a look at your UI.

Sadly, a lot of your blog commentary may be spam. I have one blog that generates many comments per day, but half of the comments are not even closely related to the articles they are commenting about. For example, I might write an article about a certain gadget, and someone will add the comment, "Nice well written article, it reminds me of Toupees for Men," along with a link to Toupees for Men, where a sale can hopefully be made. Some comments are even generated by machines. There are programs designed to sniff out sites and leave spam that's posing as legitimate commentary. Fortunately, if you use a blog service with CAPTCHA web forms and spam filters, you can stop this spamming problem before the taint becomes an infection.

Spreading the Word Through Social Media

I mentioned social networking back in Chapter 4, and how you can start a Facebook site and Twitter subscription based on your application. Now, it is time to make them work for you.

Twitter

Hopefully, you took my advice in Chapter 4 and have started the habit of tweeting. During work on your application, you can leave tweets that inform the public of your process. By now, you have probably found a lot of people to follow, and you should have some followers yourself. You should then go to Twitter and make certain that you tweet the release date. This will cause your followers to know what to expect, sort of like the hype of a movie preview.

Although it's somewhat difficult to work with at first, you should be comfortable with Twitter on your computer and mobile device. If you want to, you can use a dedicated client app such as Twitterrific, Echofon, TweetDeck, or the official Twitter app for Android to keep track of it all. You can even head to oneforty's comprehensive Twitter apps directory at http://oneforty.com to explore all manner of Twitter tracking.

You should use Twitter like you use the comments on your blog. Figure out what potential users have to say about your application and address them directly. You can then tweet about how the app is going—microblogging is an excellent medium for addressing issues without giving away too much detail.

As you reply to comments, you put a human face on your product and show the world that you are not just a soulless machine whose only purpose is to make money. In the same manner, don't be constantly advertising and promoting your application, or you will come off as a 24/7 advertisement that people want to go away.

You will also have to balance that by remaining on topic. You don't want to start a whole series of tweets about things that have nothing to do with your application. It is all right to go off on a tangent occasionally, but too much going off topic will lead to another type of audience—or worse, no audience.

Another useful tool with Twitter is the *hashtag*. A hashtag is the pound symbol (#); it's used to mark keywords or topics in a tweet. Users put a # before relevant keywords in tweets in order to categorize those tweets for an easier search. Other Twitter users can click a hastagged word in any message and it will show them all other tweets in the category. Hashtagged words that become very popular can end up as trending topics.

■ **Note** A lot of journalists use Twitter as a source for finding new stories. Don't be surprised if you receive a message from a news organization wanting to talk about your application. It's quite possible that they heard about it on Twitter!

The important thing to understand about Twitter and other social networks is that quality is always better than quantity. It is not important how many followers you have, but rather who these followers are. It is the difference between 10,000 Facebook friends and 100 true friends.

In the same manner, you don't want to just start following people so you can be followed. You want to follow someone that you can learn from. Any Android (or even iOS) developer is fair game, since you will have to deal with similar issues. You should definitely follow publishers and journalists, as they are people of influence. Don't forget your friends and peers as well. Follow those who are following you.

You should also take the time to retweet other people's posts, especially if they are something that your audience would enjoy. The more you do this, the more others will eventually retweet yours. Think of it as Twitter karma.

You should take some time to create a Twitter list as well. This way, you can organize people into groups, and follow them with a quick glance every day. For example, you can name one group Developers, and see what is going on in the Android development community these days.

Facebook

You should then spread the word on Facebook, to all your friends, and those that have joined the Group that you have created.

By this time, you should have created a separate Facebook page for business. Once you get 25 people to like it, you can have a domain name of `www.facebook.com/your-business-name`.

Getting the word about your release date is pretty easy. Simply do the following:

1. Click your Facebook page's Edit Info link.

2. Click the Marketing link.

3. Click Send an Update.

You should use this method of spreading the word sparingly, as messages like this are broadcasted ad nauseum throughout the Internet. You don't want to overuse this.

Before your launch date is also a good time to start using Facebook Insights, a free analytics service. When you log into your Facebook page as an admin, you can click the View Insights link to view the metrics about your Facebook page. By studying this information, you can find out who is looking at what you are doing, which is information that will be helpful in the future.

Making a Video

This was something that I wanted to cover in Chapter 4, as video-sharing sites are a lot like social networks. Your video should show what your application will do, as well as highlight all its nifty features. Unfortunately, it is difficult to make a video about your application when you don't really have much to show yet, unless you can work up some sort of teaser/trailer.

If you haven't already, set yourself up an account on YouTube. You are going to need a place where you can put all your footage about your application, and you might as well do it on the most popular video-sharing site.

Making a video can be tricky, and if you put up a video that is of low quality, this can tarnish the reputation of your application. If you can get a video camera that can shoot high-definition video, you should be able to mount it on a tripod and lock it into one position so you can get some shots of your application on an Android device. One good example of a company that did this is PlayOn, as shown in Figure 8-4. The video is simply one person showing how the application works on an Android device. Not surprisingly, this is the best type of demo there is to show on video. You can watch this video at `www.youtube.com/watch?v=Ei1otuNk8oM`.

PlayOn.tv Android App demonstration

jsw522 16 videos ⊻   Subscribe

👍 Like 👎 + Add to ⌄ Share ▤   990 views

Figure 8-4. A demonstration of PlayOn.tv on Android

One thing that I have noticed about filming anything on screen is that it tends not to come across well on other screens. Have you ever noticed that in movies, things shown on a television screen don't show up well on the screen you are watching? In order to get a clear picture, the director has to edit it, often using special effects.

In the same manner, you are probably going to have to edit your video to make it at least acceptable quality. You can probably get away with putting an Android device or emulator on a clean table and showing people what the app can do. That, or you can use some sort of video footage from the computer itself.

You can then do a little narration, but you might have to do the audio track later. This goes for any sound that your application may have, if the microphone on your video camera doesn't get it.

I have some experience working with video, and it always takes longer than I think. After all, most two-hour movies take years to make. Don't make the mistake of thinking you can just knock out a video that is a few minutes long in just a few minutes. In fact, you might want to consider hiring a video service in order to film your application at work.

Once you have the video, you should definitely put it on your site so people can check out how your application works. This is especially helpful if you have an application that is difficult to explain.

Writing a Press Release

In Chapter 4 I discussed how you need to compile a list of key media people to inform about your application. Now I am going to advise you how to construct the press release.

A press release is a statement prepared for distribution to the media. In Chapter 4 I discussed the possibility of hiring a PR firm to represent your application, and if you're using one, you might want to ask your PR team to write your press release as well. Be sure to check it to see that it is accurate, complete, and persuasive.

Another important thing to think about is who will receive your press release. As a professional blogger, I receive a lot of press releases in my inbox every day. Many of them come from PR firms, and some are from these sites that send out press releases on a daily basis.

Format for a Press Release

Press releases have a format. It isn't really a standard, but journalists like me get so many of these a day that we know what to look for:

- *Company logo*: You should center your company logo centered at the top in full color. If nothing else, you want journalists to at least remember your company name, so make it prominent. Some sources say the company's name, web address, mailing address, and phone number should be at the top, but I usually see these at the bottom.

- *Title*: I've heard some sources say that the title should be in all capitals, but it should at least be in bold. It should be brief enough to explain what your application is, but if this has to be described at length, that is also fine. Try not to go over two lines.

- *Secondary title*: This is not part of the title; it should be centered but not bold. Here you can add a sentence that discusses your product in detail.

- *Date and city*: In bold, you should have the date and city of where the press release originated.

- *First paragraph*: This should give some brief detail about what the press release.

- *Second paragraph*: This is where the journalistic *who, what, where, when, why,* and *how* come in. In your case, you should put in who cares, why you should care, where one can find it, and when it will happen.

- *Quote*: For some reason, press releases generally have a quote from someone within the company itself. I believe that it is meant to be a personal touch. The quote is usually something about how the company is "excited" to bring customers their product; you definitely want to use a genuine quote from an excited executive about the product here.

- *Final paragraph*: As a tech and gadget blogger, I always end my articles with a final paragraph that explains the price of the item, as well as any details about the point of sale.

- *Company description*: This is usually preceded by "About Shoobaha, Inc.," and discusses the company in terms of the date it was founded and what the company does. You should then put your web site URL there.

Example of a Press Release

Remember that idea I had for a baseball card organizer back in Chapter 2? Figure 8-5 shows an example of what the press release for this might look like.

Your Company Logo
Here

Baseball Card Organizer Now Available on Android Devices: Allows Users to Put Collection on Their Android Device

Card collectors can now take their collection wherever they take their Android phone or tablet

SEATTLE, WA (October 31, 2011): Shoobaha, a company known for creating applications on various mobile platforms, announced today the availability of the Baseball Card Organizer application for Android. The application allows the user to put their baseball card collection on their phone or tablet with the use of the camera on their Android device.

Baseball Card Organizer includes a built-in database that allows the user to photograph the front of the card, as well as the back with the stats. The user can then enter in information, and organize the cards alphabetically or by team.

This allows the user to take their baseball card collection with them without taking their collection with them. He or she can then flip through their cards by flicking on the screen. Baseball Card Organizer is also good for organizing other types of cards, such as movie trading cards.

"Most people who collect baseball cards have to keep them in protected cases, and they don't have the fun of flipping through them without degrading their condition," said Jack Jackson, cofounder of Shoobaha. "Baseball Card Organizer gives the user the fun of perusing their collection and not worrying about getting sweat on their investment. Best of all, the user can do this from anywhere."

The Baseball Card Organizer application is now available on the Android Market, as well as the company web site, at www.shoobaha/samplecompany.com. The Baseball Card Organizer Lite is free, but the full version costs $0.99.

About Shoobaha:

Shoobaha was started as a startup company in 2010, devoted to making applications for all mobile devices. Since its launch, Shoobaha has created many applications, including More Useful Stuff, Helpful Applications, and More Terrific Applications.

Notice in the end how I took advantage of the press release to advertise other applications. I also took the time to highlight the best features, and included a quote about the app. This is meant to be read by someone in the reporting business and make it easier for them to write an article about the app.

Employing Other Creative Marketing Strategies to Reach Your Audience

As you can see, there are a lot of ways to create a prerelease buzz for your Android application. But don't be afraid to think outside the box as well.

Let me give you an example. Right now, I am in the process of working on an application. I don't want to get into what it is exactly, for legal reasons that I discussed in Chapter 3, but I can tell you it is software that helps users prepare for tests.

My main target audience is going to be students, both at the high school and college levels. Fortunately, I happen to live in a college town, and I am less than eight miles away from another college.

My plan is to create colorful fliers that look similar to the web presence that I have previously shown in Figures 8-1 and 8-2 above. I could make these fliers 8×14 inches so I would have plenty of room to add more content if I saw fit. Even before the app is created, I could get the poster made, with a small space reading "Coming Soon." I could then put the posters all over the college campuses so that students will know that there is an application to help them with their studies.

Once the application is made and out on the market, I could then make more of the same posters, but instead of "coming soon," I would include a QR code showing where to get the application. I will explain more about QR codes in Chapter 10, but in essence, these allow users to download the application directly from the poster via the user's bar code application.

As you can see, I figured out a marketing campaign that involves the use of nothing more than posters, and will reach the audience that needs it. I will have to figure out where to put the fliers so college students will see them. Not only is it important where I put the fliers up, but when. For example, if I put up these fliers at the beginning of the school year, they will be ignored, because students aren't generally thinking about studying for tests at this time. However, as it gets toward finals week, an application that helps one study will look very good to the students.

This is what a marketing campaign is all about: reaching the right audience, in the right place, at the right time. When considering a grassroots marketing campaign such as the one just explained, try to think about the culture referred to in Chapter 3, figure out where they are, and meet them where they are at. For example, if there are conventions related to your application, then make plans to go there. (I will discuss conventions in more detail in Chapter 11.)

Summary

Before your application is launched, there is a lot to do to prepare for its release. There are several places where you will want to spread the word about your new application.

You should set up your web site so the release date is prominent, and make certain that it is set up so future sales can be made once the application becomes available. You should write more blogs about the application so that RSS followers will stay updated about your application.

In addition to blogging and updating the web site, it is also time to spread the word about the imminent application with Twitter and Facebook, as well as other social media sites. You should also make a video of your application in action so it can be posted on YouTube and other video sites.

Take the time to make a press release to distribute to those in the media that will report on your application. You should also consider other methods of marketing that are unconventional in order to reach your target audience.

CHAPTER 9

Publishing to the Android Market

This chapter is going to be exciting, as I will present everything you need to know about getting your application on the Android Market at last. I am going to assume that your application is running without error, which is necessary for publishing to the Market. I'm sure that you have discovered that getting the application to run without errors is just the beginning. You might find that your application does exactly what you programmed it to do, but still not what you want it to do.

Eventually, you have to meet your launch date deadline, and if you can't get the application to be perfect, you should at least have it running smoothly. If you don't get everything you want on your application, relax! You can always update it later, and I will explain how to do that in the next chapter.

As I said in Chapter 1, submitting to the Android Market is easier than the Apple App Store because there isn't any approval process. That means that you don't have to sit around and wait for Apple (or Google) to get back to you. That also means that shortly after you are finished with all of the steps in this chapter, your application will be ready for downloading by Android users around the globe.

This is where it gets pretty exciting, as you are about to have a grand opening for your application. The potential for users and profits awaits, and your application will be available for review on the Android Market. You had better make certain that it is worthy of five stars!

This also means that you will need to shift gears as far as marketing is concerned, as you go from prerelease buzz to post-release buzz. That is something that I will go into detail about in the next chapter, but for now, I want to briefly address those who are entering the Android Market for the first time.

Is This Your First Android Application?

If it is, then you might want to hold off on your marketing. Marketing is all about showing people your best product, so people will fall in love with it and want it for their own. If your product is mediocre, then the relationship could be over before it even starts.

This was the case for my first application. I knew that I wanted it out by a certain time, but I just couldn't meet that deadline. I also could not get some of my desired features to work. Part of the problem was that the features needed to wait for certain information that I wouldn't have until a few weeks later. Some of the features wouldn't work because I couldn't figure out how to program them. Even though I didn't want to do this, I put a disclaimer in TextView on the splash screen that read, "This application is still under construction. More features are coming soon. Please do not review yet."

Even though that disclaimer is somewhat unprofessional, you can probably see why I did that. The last thing I want is someone giving me a one-star review for my application when I can't finish it properly. I made sure that the buttons that would have opened a terrific feature opened a window that said, "This feature is coming soon."

Eventually, I was able to make the updates necessary to alter the application, and when all the activities worked, I felt that I could take down my "pardon our dust" disclaimer. In other words, I didn't turn up the marketing until I had something I could brag about. Of course, if you are working for someone else, you may not have that option. If that is the case, then you may have to miss a deadline just to get the application running at full capacity. I hope your boss understands.

What to Do Before You Submit to the Android Market

Here is what you want to have sorted out in advance on your application before you submit it to the Android Market:

- The application should run without any bugs. This may sound obvious, but it is sometimes difficult to find them. The last thing you need is an application that has even one "Force Close" window. If this kind of error happens even once, your users could give your application a one-star rating. Before you submit to the Android Market, you will want to test every button, feature, and activity to make certain that it runs without a problem. You also might want to do a round of beta testing; I will go into detail on this in the next chapter.

- Test it out in portrait and landscape mode. You might have a terrific application that looks awesome, but you had better make certain that it looks just as awesome when you turn your Android device sideways. Auto-landscape is a great built-in feature for Android, but it may inadvertently distort your application's look. It is possible for a developer to turn off this feature. Your emulator is able to show you what your application looks like in both views, and make certain you get a good look at your application on a few actual Android devices and Android versions before you do an official release.

- Make it easy for someone to give you a review. If you have a good application, and you think it is worthy of five stars, then you will want to make certain that the user can easily give you the rating that you feel you richly deserve. You can set up the application to prompt the user to give you are review. See Chapter 5 for how to set that up.

- If you have other apps, set up your own in-app store. If you and your company have other applications that you want to sell, then you should set up that store before officially releasing. Also check Chapter 5 if you want to learn more on that.

- Set up your ads. If you want to maximize your profits, you want to make certain that those ads are in place with AdMob, Mobclix, or whatever ad method you decided to go with. See Chapter 6 for how to set that up.

- Have your in-app billing set up. This is for those who are planning on promoting other applications within their own applications, as well as planning to put a market within their application. See Chapter 7 for how to set that up.

- Have a good description set up. Your Android application is required to have a description that is less than 4,000 characters. It would be wise to have one that is well thought out, rather than one that sounds like you winged it.

- Get some good screenshots ready. I will detail how to get a decent screenshot for your application in this next section.

How to Obtain a Screenshot of Your Android Device

Part of the process of submitting to the Android Market includes taking screenshots of your app. You are allowed eight of them, and these will appear on the official entry of your application on the Android Market. You should use all eight of them if you can. Also, you should have a video ready (I discussed how to make a video in Chapter 8).

When it comes to screenshots, you do not want to use anything that isn't pulled off the screen of the application itself. You need to show potential users precisely what they will be getting when they download your application.

Sometime during your testing, you should be using an Android device as your personal emulator (I discussed how to set this up in Chapter 1). Here is what you are going to do to get a screenshot from it:

1. Connect your Android device to your computer.

2. Open up the android-sdk folder, wherever you have saved it.

3. Open up the tools folder (see Figure 9-1).

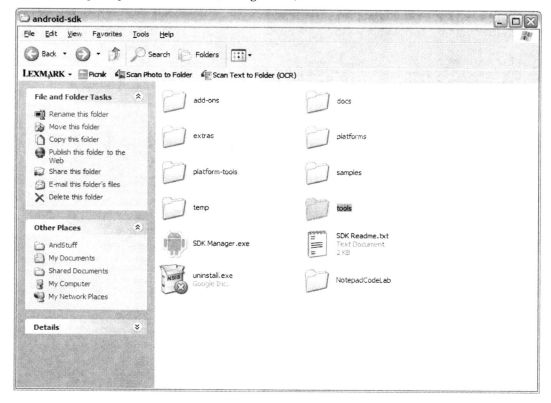

Figure 9-1. *What you should find when opening the android-sdk folder (provided you are a Windows XP user)?*

4.   Click the MS-DOS batch file known as `ddms.bat` (see Figure 9-2).

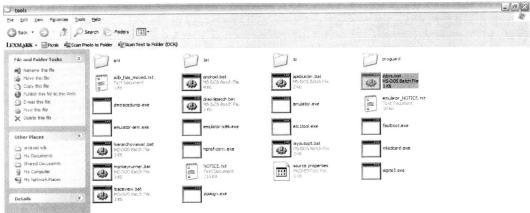

Figure 9-2. *The android-sdk tools folder, where you will find the important ddms.bat file necessary to get a screenshot*

5.   Open the Dalvik Debug Monitor. You should see your Android device recognized. Click the device. (In Figure 9-3, it is the one that is running Gingerbread, a version designated by the number 2.3.3.)

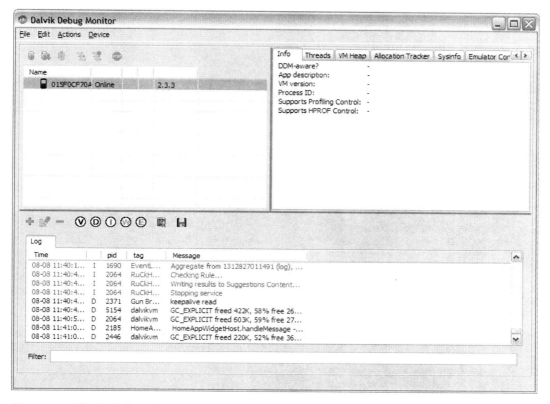

Figure 9-3. *The Dalvik Debug Monitor, which you will need in order to get a screenshot for your application*

6. If your Android device has shut off, turn it on, unlock it, and make certain that the screen you want is ready.

7. Select Device, and then select Screen Capture.

8. As you can see from Figure 9-4, you will have a perfect screenshot of what is on the screen of the Android device at that given moment.

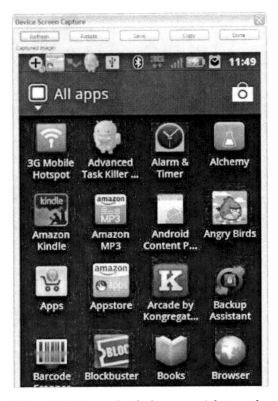

Figure 9-4. *A sample of what you might see when you get your screenshot. This one is my home screen.*

9. Click Save and designate a place to save the image file. Make certain that you know where that is, as you will need it later.

Selecting the Proper Screenshot

We all know the old cliché about how a picture is worth a thousand words, and most Android users "read" the pictures of your application on the Android Market, rather than reading the description. It is important for developers to put their best photos forward when it comes to screenshots.

In other words, don't just go through your application and take screenshots of the main menu screen. Your aim is to try and find the best visual example of your application in action. For this reason, you may not want to use the menu screen, since the menu screen is usually a motionless layout of buttons. What you are looking for are screenshots that show your application in motion. If you have a gaming application, then you want to show a very exciting level. The key is to tell a story with your screenshots.

Figure 9-5 shows the screenshots for the Android Market entry of Burn the Rope. Burn the Rope is a very addictive game where the player must burn a rope in its entirety by making the flame burn upward. This is done by twisting the Android device; the accelerometer senses the direction you are holding the phone or tablet and responds accordingly. In addition to burning rope for a higher score, you also earn points by burning insects that are on the rope.

App Screenshots

Figure 9-5. *Screenshots for Burn the Rope on the Android Market. Can you tell why they were chosen?*

The screenshot on the left of Figure 9-5 is one that is used as a transition scene in the game. Here, the Android user sees what the game is all about: a flame taking on bugs. This is the promise of fun game conflict, and one that is most unusual. The two images on the right show what the game play is all about. In the center screen you can see multiple flames burning, along with bugs who are about to get singed. Altogether, these images show potential users that they are about to play a pyromaniac's game of bug-killing skill.

In the same manner, you will want to show screenshots from your application that will show it in action. I realize that this might be difficult if your application isn't an action-packed game like Burn the Rope. You should then think what features you are boasting about, and find a screenshot that exemplifies them. For example, if you are selling a document scanner that uses the Android device's camera, use a screenshot showing the camera view of a document being scanned, with the text "Click camera to scan the document."

Notice that you might have to alter the programming code a bit in order get a decent screenshot. Sometimes this is necessary so you don't have a screenshot that looks dull and boring. When your application is on the Android Market, you want screenshots that are visually compelling. You want a user to look at them and say, "Oh, I see what it is; I have got to download that."

You also will need to make certain that your screenshots are the proper dimensions and file format. The Android Market specifies 320×480, 480×800, 480×854, or 1280×800 in 24-bit PNG or JPEG. I had no trouble getting the proper dimensions with the ddms.bat file, which gave me an instant 480×854 screenshot from my Droid X. Hopefully, you will achieve the correct results just as easily, but if not, you might need to adjust your photos with a program like Microsoft Picture Viewer.

How to Create a Distributable File

Now that you have your screenshots ready, you should also prepare an Android Package (APK) file. There are a few ways you can do this, but the one I will be focusing on is through the ADT inside the Eclipse IDE. If you did not use Eclipse to create your Android application, then you can use an automated build process, such as Hudson Continuous Integration Server. You can find out more about that at http://hudson-ci.org.

Eclipse automatically signs the Android application and compiles it in the APK file. (If you want to learn more about these packaging methods, then go to `http://d.android.com/guide/publishing/app-signing.html`.)

To publish on Android, you must digitally sign your file with certification that has a public/private key pair. Let me repeat this for emphasis: *your Android application must be signed.*

When it is time to release the application to the market, you must sign it in with a private key. You as the developer will have this key, and this certification is used to sign the application, which is in turn used to identify the application. The certificate is used to identify the author of an application, as well as establish a trust relationships between applications. It is possible to use self-signed certificates for signing your applications.

You may have noticed when you are checking your workspace files out that there is already an APK file there. This is because while you are developing and testing, you can compile in debug mode. The build tools use the Keytool utility included within the JDK to create a *keystore* with a known alias and password. The keystore is the container where your personal certificates are. During each compiling, the tools use the debug key to sign the application APK file.

You can use ADT tools to generate the certificate, and I will explain how to do that in the next section. If you don't want to do it through Eclipse, another option is using standard tools like Keytool or Jarsigner in order to sign APK files. With the Keytool and Jarsigner approaches, you must first compile your application to an unsigned APK, and then sign the APK manually to generate your own private key using Jarsigner (or another similar tool). If you don't have a private key already, you can then run Keytool manually to generate your own keystore/key, and sign into the application with Jarsigner.

Fortunately, Eclipse allows the user to create a keystore file. This is what Android uses to identify your application on the Android Market. I will go into detail on that on the next section, and I will assume that you programmed your application on Eclipse as opposed to another type of tool. If you want more information on signing your applications, you can learn more at `http://d.android.com/guide/publishing/app-signing.html`.

Creating an APK File Using Eclipse

The following exercise walks you through creating an APK file using Eclipse:

1. Open Eclipse, and choose the proper workspace for your application.

2. Right-click the app name at the top of Package Explorer, as shown in the highlighted section in Figure 9-6.

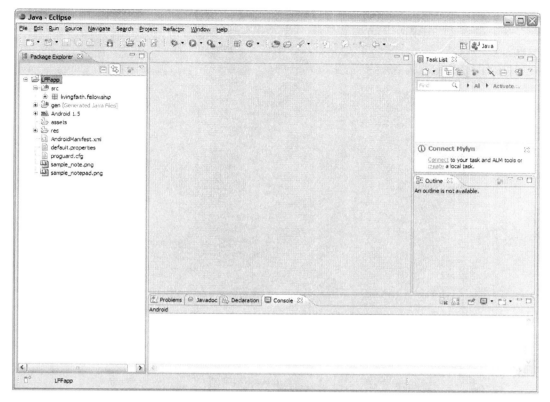

Figure 9-6. *A completed Android program—a prerequisite for submitting your application to the Android Market. Note that there are no red Xs, which means the program is running without errors.*

3. Choose Android Tools, and then choose Export Signed Application Package. Notice that there is an option for Export Unsigned Application Package. You don't want to use that now. When you pick the Export Signed Application Package, you should see a window that looks just like Figure 9-7. Verify that you have the right project selected, and click Next.

Figure 9-7. What you will see after you export your signed application package

4. Here you will need to set up a keystore for the first time, assuming you have not done it already. You will then see the window in Figure 9-8.

▪ **Note** Just like your house keys, you should have a copy of your keystore safely backed up somewhere. You should make a compressed or zipfile of your keystore and save it in a secure and easily locatable place on your computer.

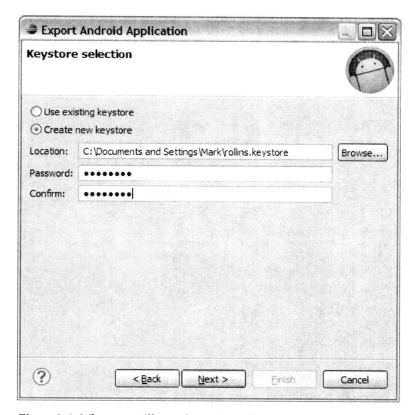

Figure 9-8. What you will see when using a keystore

5. Check "Create new keystore." You will now need to enter a location on your hard drive for where you want your keystore. I put mine where my workspaces are for Eclipse, which makes it easier to remember. Pick a password that you can easily remember, and confirm it.

6. If you already have a keystore, you now just need to choose the correct alias. I go into more detail on this in Chapter 11. For now, go ahead and click Finish, and you will see the window shown in Figure 9-9.

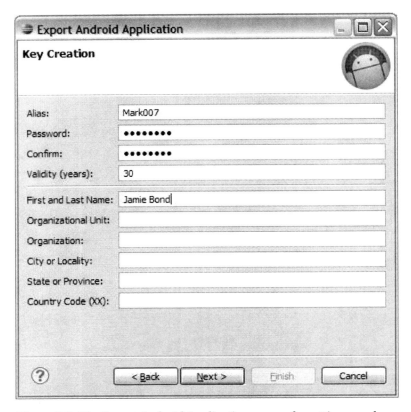

Figure 9-9. The Export Android Application screen, for setting up a key

7. Now it's time to enter an alias. In this example, I chose Mark007 for fun. Then you must enter a password specifically for the alias, and again reconfirm it. As for the validity, this key is designed to expire after October 22, 2033. According to the Android Developers site, the market server "enforces the requirement to ensure that users can seamlessly upgrade Market applications when new versions are available." Since many of the sites recommend choosing 30 years, this is what I used, as you can see.

8. Next, enter your first and last name, and fill in the Organizational Unit, Organization, City or Locality, State or Province, and Country Code (XX) fields. A country code is a two-letter code supplied by the International Organization for Standardization (ISO). You can find a list of them all at www.worldatlas.com/aatlas/ctycodes.htm.

9. Click Next, and you will see the screen shown in Figure 9-10.

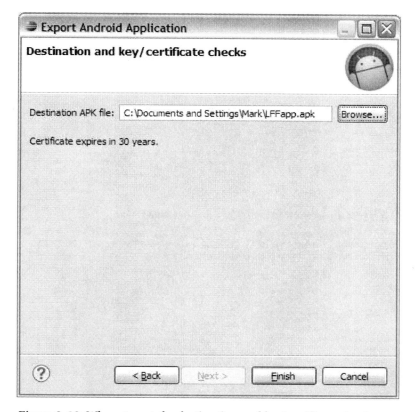

Figure 9-10. Where to put the destination and key/certificate checks

10. Click Finish, and go ahead and enter the path where you want to keep your keystore.

Creating an Account on the Android Market

It is now time to publish your application to the Android Market. You will need to use this URL: http://market.android.com/publish.

From here, you will need to sign in with a Google account, and I would high recommend using a Gmail account. I brought up in Chapter 4 how you should have a business e-mail address, and this is the time to use it.

Go on and sign in with your Google username and password. If you don't have an account, click the "Create an account now" link to set one up, as shown in Figure 9-11.

Figure 9-11. *You will need a Google account if you want to sign into the Android Market.*

You will need to create a developer profile, and it would be wise to have your credit card ready to pay the registration fee. After you sign in, you should see a screen like Figure 9-12.

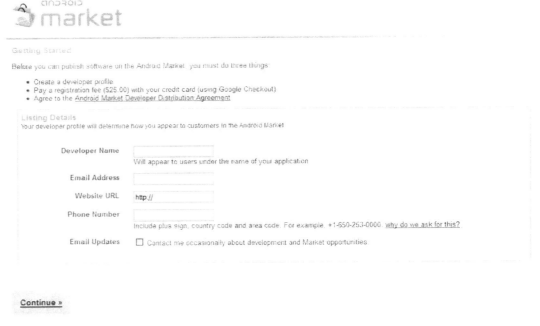

Figure 9-12. *Before you can publish, you need to fill out the developer profile page.*

Fill in all the appropriate information. You can use your own name or your company name for the applications that you release. It can be changed later if you want.

If you want to use the same Gmail address that you used to log in, then it is quite easy. The e-mail address appears by default in the Email Address window. If you choose not to use this e-mail address, then you can type in whatever e-mail address is best for you.

Check the Email Updates box if you want to receive updates; otherwise, skip it and just click Continue, and you will see a screen like Figure 9-13.

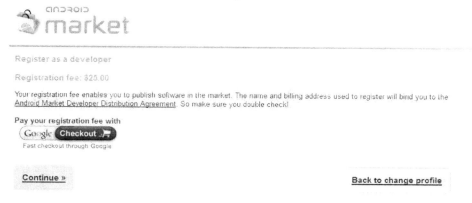

Figure 9-13. A warning before you pay the registration fee

Now you come to the payoff. Actually, this is where you will be paying Google off. If you are in the habit of shopping online, it will be quite easy. In fact, if you have a credit card on file with Google, you might not see a screen where you fill out your credit card information. Figure 9-14 is what I saw when I registered for my account, explaining that the card that I was using on my Google account had expired. If this is your first time, you will be seeing the usual fill-in-the-blanks for when you make an online purchase.

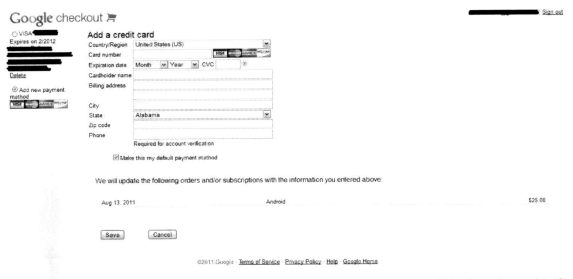

Figure 9-14. *You will need to fill out a form for personal billing information. It will look similar to this if it is your first time registering a credit card on a Google account.*

Fill out the form and then click Continue or Checkout to pay. (I clicked on both Continue and Checkout and got the same result.) Read the terms of service and click Agree; then click Continue, and you will see a screen like Figure 9-15.

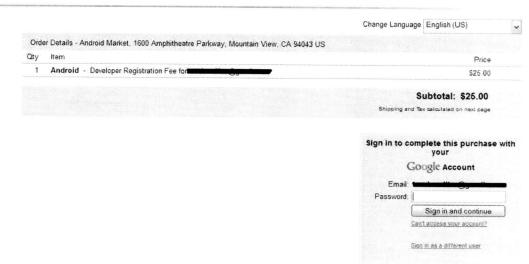

Figure 9-15. After you fill out the information to pay the fee, you will be asked to sign in again.

You will then see a screen that will ask you for your password again, and then you will see an order confirmation screen like in Figure 9-16. Click the check boxes on the left if you want to receive special offers, keep your e-mail address confidential, and/or receive promotional Android e-mails, or just click the "Place your order now" button.

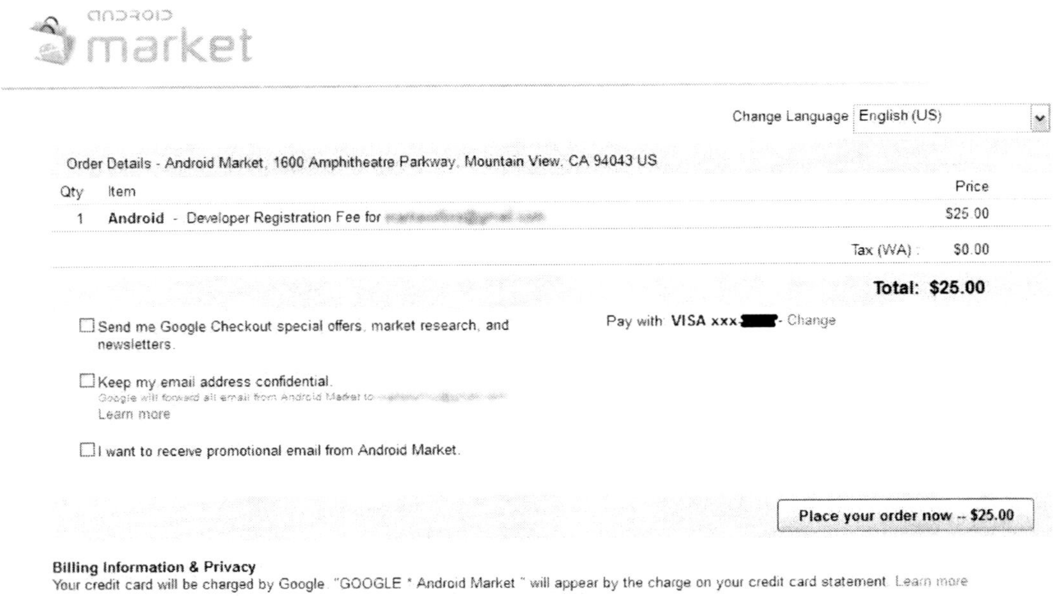

Change Language: English (US)

Order Details - Android Market, 1600 Amphitheatre Parkway, Mountain View, CA 94043 US

Qty	Item	Price
1	**Android** - Developer Registration Fee for ~~~~~~~~~~~~~~~~	$25.00
	Tax (WA) :	$0.00

Total: $25.00

☐ Send me Google Checkout special offers, market research, and newsletters.

Pay with **VISA xxx**▆▆- Change

☐ Keep my email address confidential.
Google will forward all email from Android Market to ~~~~~~~~~~~~~~~
Learn more

☐ I want to receive promotional email from Android Market.

[Place your order now -- $25.00]

Billing Information & Privacy
Your credit card will be charged by Google. "GOOGLE * Android Market " will appear by the charge on your credit card statement. Learn more

Figure 9-16. The order details screen, which is not the same as the confirmation screen. One more step is required.

You will see a confirmation screen for your order like the one in Figure 9-17. However, you're not quite done yet.

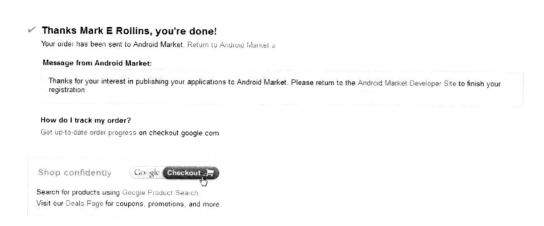

Figure 9-17. *An order confirmation saying that you are done. All this means is that you have paid for the privilege of using Android, and you can now post your applications to the market.*

You will want to click Android Market Developer Site to finish your registration. Here you will find the Android Market Developer Distribution Agreement, as shown in Figure 9-18.

Figure 9-18. *The Android Market Developer Distribution Agreement terms page*

■ **Caution** Take the time to read over the agreement before continuing. If you violate this agreement, Google might shut you down before you have a chance to fix the issues with your application.

After you've read over the agreement, click the "I agree" check box. You will then see a window saying that you can upload to the Android Market, as shown in Figure 9-19.

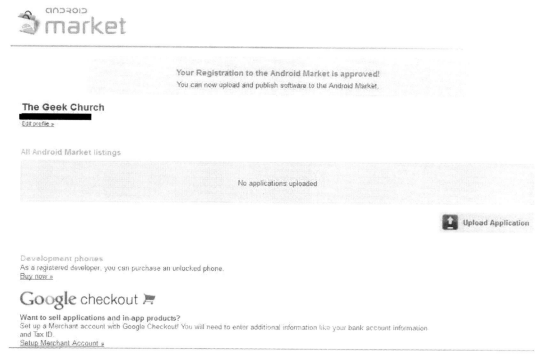

Figure 9-19. *What you will see on the Android Developers home page. You are now ready to begin uploading applications.*

Uploading Your Application

You should be able to click the blue area marked "Upload Application" to start the process of officially uploading the application. You should see the screen that you see in Figure 9-20. If you have navigated away from this screen, just go back to `http://market.android.com/publish`.

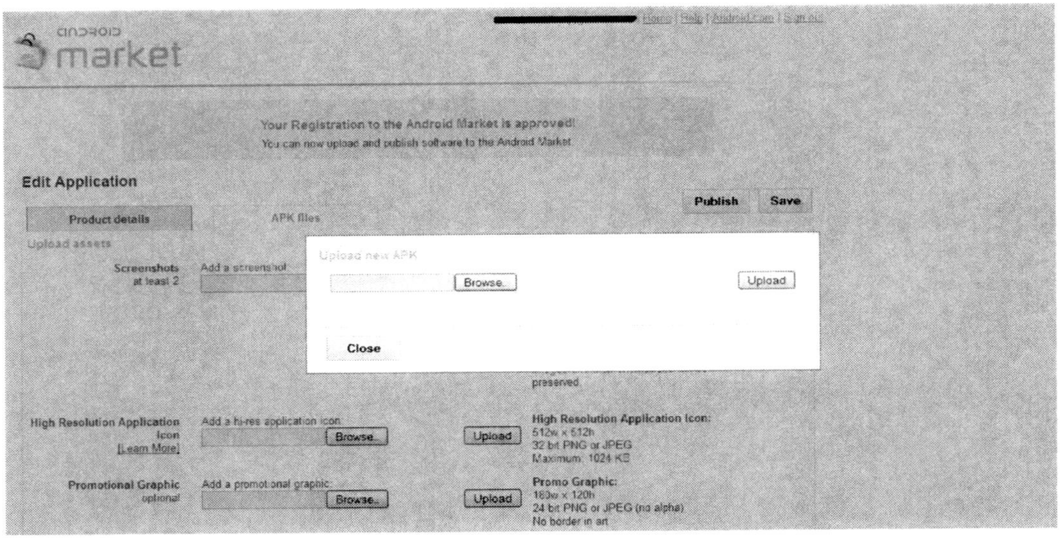

Figure 9-20. *Time to upload your APK*

You will then need to upload the application that you just unlocked in your keystore. Be certain that the name you want for the application is the same name as the APK file. If you want to change the name of the APK file, you should do that before you upload it. When it is loaded, you should see something like Figure 9-21.

Figure 9-21. *What you should see after your APK is loaded. Note that the icon is clearly visible.*

Now you will need to upload a variety of other items for your app, as shown in Figure 9-22.

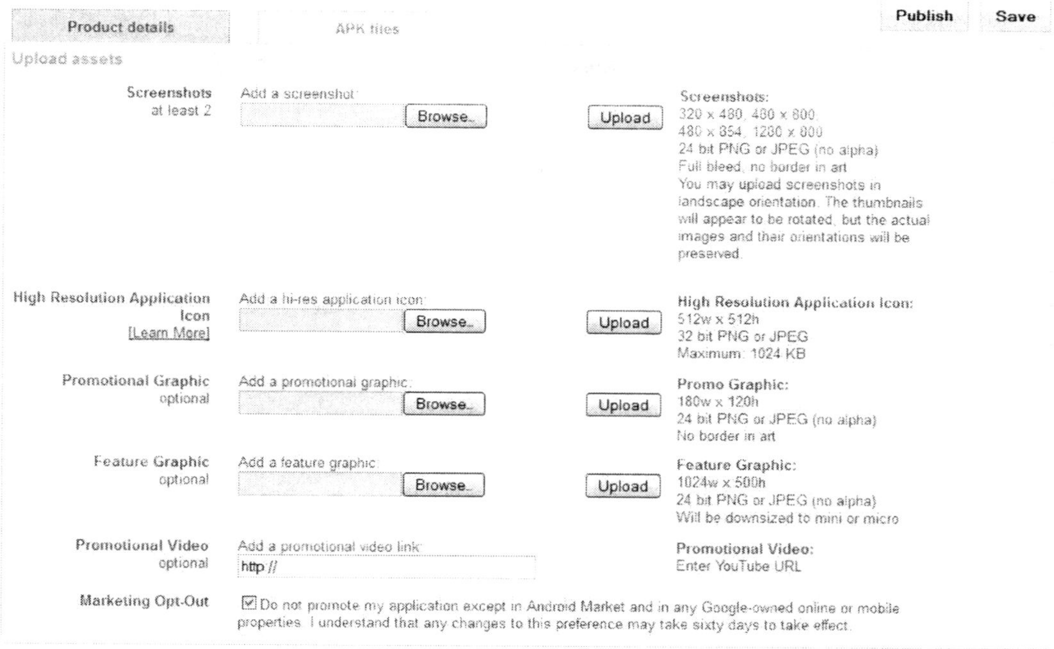

Figure 9-22. The "Upload assets" area

You will then need to upload the screenshots from wherever you saved them on your computer; you will see these screenshots very clearly after they are uploaded. I discussed earlier in this chapter the proper dimensions of a screenshot and what kinds of shots you'll want to include, so take a look back if you need a refresher. As of November 2010, the Android Market allows for eight possible screenshots, so you should make the most of them.

As shown in Figure 9-22, you are required to submit a high-resolution icon, which will appear in various locations in the Android Market. It is not meant to replace your launcher icon; note that its dimensions are relatively large in comparison (512×512).

The promotional graphic is different from the screenshots, and it will only show on the Android Market on devices with version 1.6 or later. According to the official Android Market site, this will be in use in various locations in the Android Market, and that is about as specific as it gets. This is completely optional, but you have hopefully created a lot of promotional material for your application, so you might as well use it here.

The feature graphic will be used on the Android Market, and it "will be downsized to mini or micro," according to the Android Market help section. The specs are officially spelled out as 1024w×500h, 24-bit PNG or JPEG, with no transparency. Also required is a safe frame of 924×400 with 50-pixel padding on each side. The feature graphic can be the application's official logo, combined with any official graphics. Android recommends large font sizes and a simple graphic, as it could be scaled down from the original size. Like the promotional graphic, the feature graphic is optional.

The promotional video is another optional step that I recommend doing. I already discussed the basics of a promotional video in the last chapter as part of generating prerelease buzz. The Android

Market requires you to use a YouTube video in this case; you can simply copy and paste your YouTube video URL into the Promotional Video field.

The marketing opt-out allows you to choose not to have your application feature in whatever promotions Google may run for the Android Market. You should check the Marketing Opt-Out box if you want Google to use your application in any sort of promoting.

The next section is for the listing details, as shown in Figure 9-23.

Figure 9-23. *The "Listing details" section of the Android Market publishing form*

The first step in this section is merely deciding what language you want your listing in. It automatically defaults to English in the United States. This was good for my first application, as it was designed for a specific audience in the United States. If you really want your application to succeed worldwide, though, then you need to think globally. Set it for any language of any country that will use your application. This does not mean that your program will necessarily work in these other countries, though, as certain APIs (such as those from Yahoo) only work in the United States. You will probably want to test out your application in other countries with various Android users to make certain it works.

The Title section is where your application finally gets a name. I discussed this in Chapter 2, and hopefully you have finally settled on one that is short, sweet, and memorable. Perhaps you have taken it a step further and bought the domain so you can use it as the URL of your web site. Also make certain that the name of your application will be easily found by a search engine.

Like naming a child, you have to settle on something, and here is the moment of truth. If you are marketing free and paid versions, don't forget to put "free" or "lite" if it is a free application, or "plus" if it is a paid one (or whatever you are planning to name these if you are using this popular Android marketing strategy).

The Description field allows you to enter a 4,000-character description of your application. If this isn't enough space for you, you can use the Recent Changes section to add more content. Your description should be a brief, easy-to-read overview of all your application's best features.

As you might have guessed, you don't have to deal with the Recent Changes section if this is your first time. In the next section, I will talk about what to do when you need to update your application. Here you can list what is new in your application, but for now, leave it blank.

You only have to worry about the Promo Text section if you are using a promotional graphic. (In fact, if you try to type in this field without a promotional graphic, you will get an error message when you try to publish). This promo text will appear when a user clicks the promotional graphic.

As I discussed in Chapter 2, you will have to eventually choose an application category. It is a difficult choice, and it narrows it with games or applications. The Games section has different categories:

- Arcade and Action

- Brain and Puzzle

- Cards and Casino

- Casual

- Racing

- Sports Games

Personally, I would have preferred more categories on the game front, as some of the best games defy a genre-naming convention. If that's the case for your application, just choose a category and run with it.

The next section deals with publishing options (see Figure 9-24).

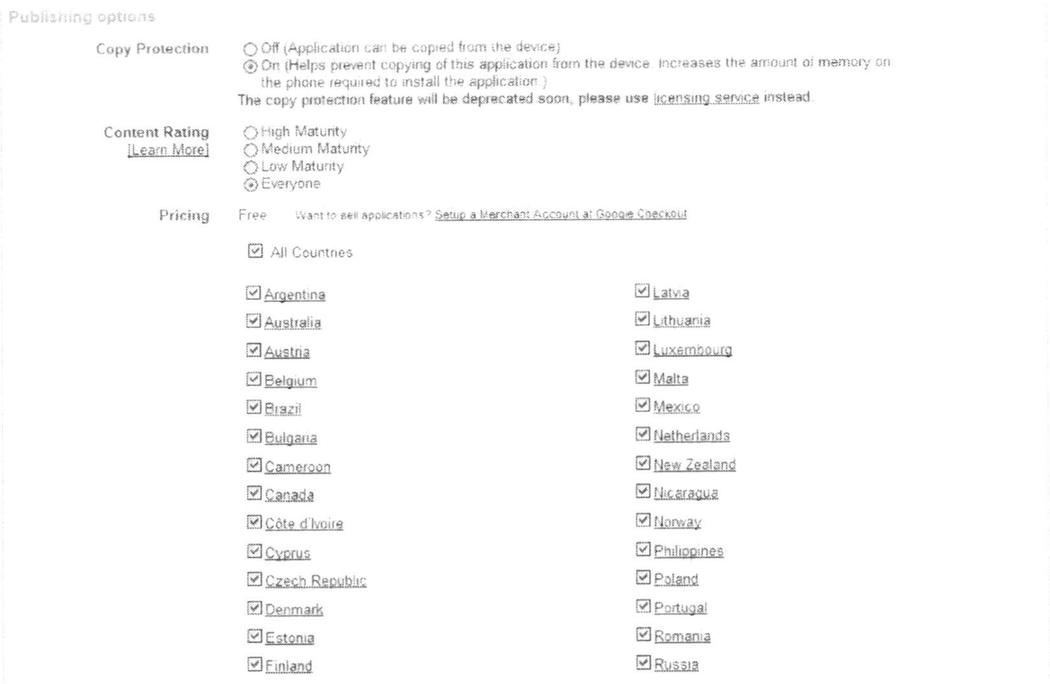

Figure 9-24. The "Publishing options" section of the Android Market publishing form

When it comes to copy protection, many of my sources say to choose the Off option, as the On option doubles the size of the APK file. The reason this section is here is because before Froyo (version 2.2), Android users could not install applications on their SD card. You should probably keep your file size as small as you can, so Off is the best option if you have a program that takes up a lot of memory. Now, if your file takes up little memory, and you are concerned about copy protection, go ahead and choose On.

You will then need to rate the content of your application, and you have four choices:

- Everyone

- Low Maturity

- Medium Maturity

- High Maturity

Notice that there is a link there that will take you to page that goes into great detail about what level your application should be rated. Factors include the following:

- Alcohol, tobacco, and drug use

- Gambling

- Profanity and crude humor

- Sexual and suggestive content

- User-generated content and user-to-user communication

- Violence

If your application contains any of these things, make sure you have it set for the proper rating, according to the Android Market. This is one rule that you really want to follow, as a violation of it could cause you to be flagged as incorrectly rated, and it will be then re-rated. Google states that "Repeat offenders may be subject to further action, up to and including account termination." In other words, Google is serious about not wanting certain stuff on their Android applications.

From there, it is time to list the price. Chapter 6 discusses the pros and cons of free and paid applications, so revisit that chapter if you're still unsure of what or whether you want to charge. You can then set up a merchant account by clicking the link on the Pricing line.

The list of locations really speaks for itself, and you can probably just leave all of them checked unless there is something on this application that is only good in one country. For example, a San Francisco street map application isn't going to do much good in any other country but the United States. The country list gets really complicated after the first part, as there is another checklist of countries after the first list. I am not certain why all the countries are not grouped together, but you should find whatever country you are looking for there.

You will then notice a section that says "Supported Devices" and "This application is only available to devices with these features, as described in your application manifest." I was taken aback when I saw this for the first time, especially when I saw the part saying, "This application is available to over 0 devices." My first thought was, "Uh-oh, did I do something wrong?" As a developer, these thoughts tend to go through your head sometimes. As it turns out, I had nothing to fear, as after the application was published, I saw that it had over 507 devices, and I could even click to see what devices were using it. So don't worry about what the Supported Devices section says for now.

From here, there are two sections left to be filled out. The first is for contact information, and the next is for consent, as shown in Figure 9-25.

Figure 9-25. The last two sections of the Android Market publishing form

Unless you have someone else who will handle all matters pertaining to your application, you should put your e-mail address here, along with your phone number.

Chapter 3 discussed creating a web site and blog for your application. It had better be up and running by this point, as this will appear on the Android Market in the Developer section.

As for the phone number, this is required too. Google has a link to a page explaining that you must provide your phone number so that Google can contact you should any problems arise. I'm sure you do not want to be flooded with calls in regard to your application. Believe me when I say that if your application runs smoothly, very few people will contact you to say how good it is. Chances are you'll receive calls when your application isn't working, though. These calls from users can happen any time day or night, so be prepared for that!

You should read anything that has a link in the consent section, and scroll back to the top and click Publish. If any errors are detected, you will have to go back and correct them.

The App Is Published, Now What?

Sit back and watch the profits grow, that's what! Okay, you don't want to be doing that, as you might be sitting a long time.

The first thing you should do is just check to see if your app is available on the Android Market. Go ahead and enter your application's name into the search engine.

If you don't see it on the Android Market, don't panic! This happened to me, and I first thought I had not filed correctly. Fortunately, there was a help section on the Android Market Publisher website. I sent a message to it, and I was answered within the hour. Granted, the answer wasn't really anything except telling me why the Android Market would filter my new application out on a search. This was when I discovered that some Android devices won't even show applications on the Android Market if they will not work on the device after being downloaded.

Considering that I had spent most of the night publishing the application, I decided to sleep on it and solve the problem in the morning. After I woke up, I did a search on the Android Market, and my application was waiting for me. I have no idea if my message to Android somehow fixed the problem. So if you can't download your application right away, wait a few hours to see if it shows up on the Android Market before you contact their help line.

I will discuss what to do on your launch date in the next chapter, but the first thing you should do is contact all of your friends and associates with Android devices and make certain that they can download your app. The point is that you are looking to see if your application works on every type of Android device. If it doesn't, then you might have a problem with your application on specific types of Android devices. You might want to take care of those before you send out your application into the world.

Summary

Submitting an application to the Android Market is a fairly simple matter, provided you follow the process. The first step is making certain the application runs without errors and does absolutely everything it is supposed to do. If it is your first, then you might want to hold off on your marketing until everything is in working order.

Part of the submission process is getting screenshots, and you can obtain screenshots with the SDK. Be sure to pick out screenshots that really show the application in action.

Before the application is submitted, it is necessary to prepare an APK file. You must digitally sign the APK file with a certification with a public/private key pair. This can be done in several ways, and one of them is on Eclipse, which can export a signed application package.

Once the destination and key certificate checks are done, you must create an account on the Android Market. After you sign in with a Google account and pay the $25.00 registration fee, you are free to submit applications.

From there, it is a simple matter of submitting your application by uploading the APK file and screenshots, and including a description and other pertinent information. Once your app is published, it should appear on the Android Market right away.

CHAPTER 10

Best Launch Day Ever

In the last chapter, you learned how to submit your application to the Android Market. Assuming you are following these chapters closely, your first application should now be available on the market for download by Android users everywhere. Take some time to celebrate this! No doubt you have worked quite hard to get this far.

Don't celebrate too hard, though. As much as you might want to rest on your laurels and wait for profits to roll in, that would be most unwise. Now that you have spent a great amount of time preparing for your application to go live, you still need to do the work so it is marketed to as many Android users as possible.

Chapters 4 and 8 discussed preparing for this day. Tasks such as drawing up a list of media people, writing press releases, making friends and followers on social networks, and so on are like sowing the seeds for your application. Now that your application is live, the launch day marks the time to reap the harvest. Just as farmers don't sleep during harvest time, these precious first days of your application's launch are a time to work.

I'm going to be focusing this chapter on your application's specific time of harvest. Chapter 11 will focus on how to keep marketing your application for many years afterward.

Deciding Whether to Have a Beta-Testing Phase

It is exciting to be an Android developer and have an application out on the market. That means that your work is there, and anyone can have access to it. Even though you have this great sense of accomplishment, and want to make certain that you are capitalizing on your investment, you might want to hold off on marketing for a while.

I know that is tough to do, when all you want to do is market this thing so you can get the greatest amount of profits as possible. However, remember what I said before about how bad reviews can make or break an application on the Android Market? Do you really want your application be plagued by bad reviews? Of course the answer is no, so I have to recommend the old cliché, "When in doubt, don't." Instead of emphasizing marketing your application, you might want to spend some time determining whether or not it works as well as you and the user expect it to.

When I created my first application, I did the work, had the frustration, and was anxious to get my application downloaded by as many Android users as I could. I live in a college town, and I created an application to be used by the locals there. A majority of my target audience were students at the nearby universities, and I wanted to get my application out on the market before the students arrived for the fall semester. I actually got the application out on the market before the students got back, effectively meeting my deadline.

I probably should have marketed the heck out of it with a flier campaign, but I deliberately held back. The reason why is that I wanted to see how well the application worked in the real world. Therefore, I found several friends who are Android users, and I asked them to try out the application.

As it turns out, it was right for me to hesitate, as I learned several things from this beta-testing phase. For example, I wanted to see if my app would work on multiple Android devices. I also wanted to know if all of those features that I spent so much time on were even usable.

For example, I wanted one of my features to be able to download MP4 video files and MP3 audio files. It turns out the method that I was using would have worked perfectly on a web browser for a computer, but fell flat when it came to doing it on an Android application. Considering that I boasted that this audio/video downloading was one of the application's main features, I realized that more work would have to be done.

Of course, I could have discovered that for myself in the early development phase of my application building. The whole reason that you do beta testing is to discover the things that you haven't thought about when it comes to your application. When word about my application got out, I received some suggestions for features that seemed obvious, after I heard them. I began to wonder why I didn't think of them myself. As developers, we live in a world where we can only see so far, and it often takes someone on the outside to figure out what is really up.

Sometimes it is the users who know the least about the development process that give us the best advice. Developers that know the most about applications can use any Android program on instinct alone, and they might not realize how a typical Android user might view your application.

Since beta testers are doing you a favor and using their valuable time to go over your application, you should take the time to compensate them for their efforts. I realize that as a first-time developer you may be on a small budget, but you should at least let your beta testers have a free copy of your application, or something else they consider valuable. Find out some way that you can help them, as they are helping you!

In the case that I explained, I used people that I knew to be beta testers. However, this doesn't always have to be the case. In fact, it is recommended that you use people that you don't know to test out your application. The point of a beta test is to be as anonymous and impersonal as possible so you will find the viewpoint of the average Android user. You can put out a request for a beta tester on your web site's blog, not to mention your social networks on Twitter and Facebook.

You can also put out a free version of your application into the market, with a clear label of "beta" on it. Once it has gone through its beta-testing phase, you can change the name, remove the beta, and kill the app. Any negative comments will be completely expunged, and you can start clean and resubmit the application with all the changes.

After I had my group of beta testers try out my application, they showed me what was and wasn't working on my application. This enabled me to go back and make some solid improvements to the application, which increased its functionality and made it more user-friendly.

In short, I recommend a beta-test phase for your application, especially if it is your first. How long you decide to go through this phase is up to you; some applications go through beta for months before their official release.

For example, LinkedIn, the professional network mentioned earlier in this book, has an official application for Android (see Figure 10-1). The beta version was released in December of 2010, but the official version didn't get official release until April 2011. Even though most people wanted an official LinkedIn application in December of 2009, it is good that the company went through the beta phase in order to find out exactly what worked and what did not work on its mobile version.

LinkedIn has over 1 million downloads as of August 2011. If it hadn't gone through its testing phase, it might have had fewer, as many users would have rejected it due to problems, regardless of whether it had the LinkedIn brand.

Linked in® **for Android™**

or **Manually Install**

Figure 10-1. LinkedIn for Android spent over four months in beta. Even though LinkedIn users probably wanted it earlier, the testing phase served to make it better.

If you are sketchy about leaving your application on the Android Market before it is ready, don't fret. I guarantee that few people will notice your application without any marketing. You don't want to let this testing phase go on too long, though, and you should set a specific date for your grand opening just like you set your launch date.

When I say "grand opening," I am referring to how new stores will open and accept customers on one date, but will have their grand opening a few days or weeks later, even though the store has technically been open before the grand opening date. Consider the beta-test phase your opening day, and your grand opening the day your beta testing ends. Then you can really shift gears on marketing, begin contacting all your press contacts, and so on.

You Have a Million Calls to Make

This is not quite accurate. If you truly want to tell everyone about your application, then you have a few billion calls to me. However, do you really think that calling every man, woman, and child on planet earth is a valid or even possible marketing strategy?

Of course not—that is why you should have started a list of media contacts, as explained in Chapter 4. You should have added a lot people to that list, and you should have created a press release, as discussed in Chapter 8. You should also have set up your social networking sites and Twitter so you can inform the greatest amount of people in the least amount of time.

Sending Out Press Releases

Hopefully you have given those press releases some revisions, and you can finally send out the polished result to a bundle of media contacts. If you want to make it easy on yourself, you can simply start a new e-mail message, and copy and paste your press release. You should use plain text e-mail format if you want media people to copy and paste your press releases to their articles. If you are unfamiliar with the world of news blogging, you should know that many online articles often include a copy of the official press release. In fact, I have worked for tech and gadget blogs that have insisted that I attach the press release to the article.

You should also include a few screenshots on the e-mail, and you also might make it easy on yourself and just use the screenshots that you used when you submitted your application to the Android Market.

You can send other types of images as well, but I would focus on images that you want to see in an online or printed journal. Every tech and gadget blog that I have written for has required me to include an image of some kind. So you definitely want to make it easy for tech reporters by finding an image that would be perfect for an article. Consider this the "cover" that readers might use to judge your "book," if I may speak in clichéd metaphors again.

This "perfect shot" doesn't have to be a screenshot; it could be a picture showing the application in use by an Android user. For example, if you have some application that improves a camera, wouldn't it be terrific to show an Android user taking a picture with your camera-improving application? The point is that you are looking for the image that will show potential users what your application is. Figure 10-2 shows an excellent example of a good image for the media.

Figure 10-2. A terrific image for an article about the Pano Android application

The image in Figure 10-2 is promotional material for Pano, an Android application that allows the user to take seamless panoramic photos without using any additional software. It is what you will see if you open up its official Android Market entry on a web browser on your computer. If I were writing an article about this application, I would use this image (and I have, actually).

The reason I would use this particular Pano image is because it has everything. The company logo is there. The slogan is there. It shows what the program does with one picture. Granted, it takes some creative liberties by showing a stretched-out Android device, but I'm certain that Android users will know that this is not one of Pano's features. For those who are interested in panoramic photos on an Android device, it will capture their attention.

The one thing that I do not recommend with your media contacts is attaching your press release and/or screenshots as e-mail attachments. As someone who has been on the other side of the table, I am less likely to open an attachment, especially if it is a PDF file. The reason is that PDF files open up Adobe Acrobat or Reader, which tends to slow down my computer a bit. Not only that, having an attached PDF is often a flag for spam filters, and you don't want your e-mail to be going there.

Here is another thing that you should know about sending out a batch e-mail to the press. You do not want to put all the names in the To section. If you do this, then all the recipients of your press release e-mail are going to see all the people that you sent it to. This looks really bad to anyone who works in the media, as it makes them feel like they are just a name on a list. Worse yet, you reveal your media contacts to everyone. What you want to do is put all your addresses in the Bcc field. This way, each recipient will receive your e-mail without seeing the others that it has been sent to. See Figure 10-3 for an example.

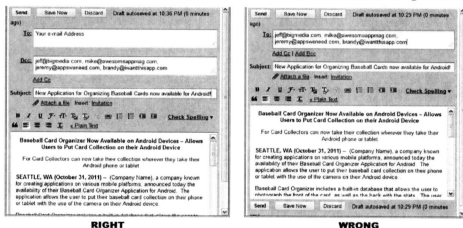

Figure 10-3. The image on the left shows how to send an e-mail of your press release to many people. Notice the recipients' addresses are in the Bcc instead of the To section.

You should also look into the option of using campaign management software. These services can handle not only e-mail marketing, but social media as well. You can run a search for "Campaign Management Software" to find many available services, and you might want to check out Constant Contact (www.constantcontact.com) and Swiftpage (www.swiftpage.com/).

Giving Your Media People a Complimentary Copy of Your Application

You will find that media reviewers are more apt to review an application if you give it to them for free.

As a tech blogger and reviewer, a product can capture my interest if its press release includes something that says, "Please let me know if we can send this to you to review." Many reviewers will say yes, as they like getting free things from time to time. Just take my word on that one.

Setting up a free sample on the Android Market is sadly not as simple as it is for Apple. Apple's App Store allows developers a "comp" code, but this is not the case for Android. Also, unless your application is on the Amazon Appstore, a gift certificate is not the best way to go. About the only way to give away a free sample is to put the APK program on your web site or make a link for it in an e-mail, after which the app can then be downloaded to the recipient's Android device.

Even though this seems like you are buying a review in exchange for a free sample, it is not. You have no guarantee that the reviewer will give you a good review simply because he or she received something for nothing. As a tech reviewer, I would never agree to any deal that said that I had to give a positive review of any review model sent to me. (In fact, no company has ever had the audacity to offer me such a deal).

In addition to giving away free samples, it is important to maintain a good working relationship with your media contacts. After all, these are the people who are doing you a favor by giving your application some much-needed press. The least you can do for them is send a thank you note for publishing your article. You don't necessarily need to make every media person your best friend, but at least establish a LinkedIn contact.

As someone who has worked as a tech and gadget blogger, I have found that I have entered into strange relationships with tech companies and their public relations team. There is sort of an unspoken rule that allows the company to give the tech reviewer something, and the tech reviewer publishes an article in return. Think of it as a quid pro quo relationship, but the reporter can only give an honest review. If the product is not of the best quality, then the review will reflect that. Therefore, send out your best product to the media, or suffer the consequences of a bad review that could be worse than any bad review on the Android Market. As a tech writer, I have often received products that are so good that I have contacted the app makers just so I could review more of what they have to offer.

Media people often get bored of looking at the same places for news stories time and time again. Sometimes they like to find a unique story for themselves, and it is helpful when these stories come via a press release.

Also, as someone who is in the media, I like to have contacts who are in the know more than I can afford to be. I keep the contact information of PR people and company representatives because they are a source for information that I may not be able to get otherwise. This book could not have been written without them, and I consulted them several times when it came to questions about developing Android applications. In other words, your developer insight could make you a good source for media people, and those media people could give you some press by quoting you. In this way, I'll occasionally contact people who I have contacted before in order to get new story ideas. Imagine if one of your media contacts sent you an e-mail saying that he or she was looking for new stories, and you just happened to be developing a new application at the time. This is certainly a better contact than a cold call to a media contact.

Setting Up a Press Room on Your Web Site

In addition to sending out several e-mails to leading people of the media, you also want to set up a virtual press room. A virtual press room allows the media people to come to you, and obtain the sources they need to write an article about your application.

You will want to set up your press room so that the user can go in and download the information he or she needs so it can be saved for later. You will also want to put the link to your press room on your home screen so it can easily be found. As you might have already guessed, you have to update this section on your web site often to keep it current.

If you don't know how to set up your web site for downloads, you are not alone. You should decide whether you want to host the files yourself or host the files externally, a decision that can be made better if you know your site's storage capacity and bandwidth. I found this site helpful for setting up downloads required for a virtual press room: `www.ehow.com/how_5869609_set-up-downloads-website.html`.

Press releases should be in DOC, RTF, or PDF format to ensure that they can be saved. Figure 10-4 shows the press information from the web site AppAware, which allows the user to find the best and newest applications by seeing what is popular for other users.

Figure 10-4. *The Press Information section on AppAware's web site. Note that a press kit is readily available for users to download with a click on the appAwarePressKit.zip link.*

I downloaded the press kit from AppAware and found that not only was it full of useful information, but images as well. You should also set up more than just press releases, as you can include screenshots, videos, company logos, the application logo, and much more.

Depending on the value of your information, you might want to make it so the media person needs a code to access the press information. I have been to many conventions and given business cards that open up a press kit on a specific URL. In many cases, I wasn't certain why the information wasn't just made public, but the code guarantees that only certain reporters can access the official and exclusive information in the press kit. The guarantees a more accurate report on the company's information.

I have found that a lot of official application web sites use the space on the press kit to do more than just give visitors access to press kits. You may have visited the press page of an application studios' web sites and found links to many articles written about the application itself.

As you have media outlets write about your application, your press page on your web site can be a sort of diary or journal where visitors can see how much your application is written about. This is something that has to be kept up, and you should do occasional searches for your application from time to time so you can link to them on your press site. You can, for example, include these in a section that says, "Here's what others have to say about us."

Using Third-Party Press Release Distribution Services

In addition to getting the word out through your media channels, you should also look into third-party press release distribution services. These distribution services charge a fee for what they do, and you definitely want to put it in your budget if you want to use these for your application.

You can find several of them by performing an online search for "press release distribution." Here are a few:

- Business Wire (`www.businesswire.com/`)

- Games Press (`www.gamespress.com/`)

- iSpreadNews (`http://ispreadnews.com`)

- Newswire (`www.newswire.net/`)

- PRWeb (`http://prweb.com`)0

- PR Newswire (`www.prnewswire.com`)

- SoftPressRelease (`www.softpressrelease.com`)

These will allow you to sign up for a specific service, and you should verify that they will distribute the press release to the news outlets that you want them to. You should also check and see what the exact price tag will be on such a service, and don't be afraid to do a little comparison shopping.

As someone who serves as a member of the press, I see e-mails from these sources in my inbox on a daily basis, and they are very helpful for finding new sources for articles.

In other words, if you use one of these services, someone from the press will see news about your application, but it may cost you. Run the numbers on your budget to see if it is worth it.

Get Your Paid Search On, If You Dare!

I did not mention the paid search part of marketing in earlier chapters, and that is simply because it is something that doesn't need a lot of preparation.

A paid search is when you pay a search engine company to provide a location for your product's web site. You may notice that when you do a Google search for something, you might see a few entries hovering above the search results. Figure 10-5 shows a search that I did for "Dog Food."

Figure 10-5. *What you will see if you run a search on "Dog Food." Note the ads before the first entries, and the ones in the right sidebar.*

What you are seeing in Figure 10-5 is someone who paid for the privilege of being featured first, even before the actual results from Google. This is because a deal has been made with Google. Anytime someone clicks this, the person or company who set the ad up (PetSmart, in this case) has to pay.

The benefits of using paid search method are obvious, as you get immediate exposure should someone be looking for your application via keywords. However, people who click these paid ads may or not buy anything when they get to your site. This would be similar to a business paying a certain amount of money for customers who may just end up looking around the store.

So while you might get the customer to see you, you won't get them to buy unless they click over to the Android Market, which is another step in the process.

In short, paid searches are a lot of money spent at a given amount of time for extra exposure, which will hopefully (emphasis on *hopefully*) give you even more exposure over time. Think of it this way: imagine paying $200 to get $400 over the next two years. Sure, you are making a profit, but it is a slow one at best. No paid search can guarantee a profit of any kind.

Paid searches are usually not recommended unless you can afford them. You might want to improve the traffic of your site with better implementation of SEO (search engine optimization) tactics, as discussed in earlier chapters. You might want to look into services like RankAssure (http://rankassure.com/) to help you out with that.

If you are a developer working for a bigger company, then you might want to make recommendations to your employer for paid searches. If that is the case, then check out AdWords (see Figure 10-6). This service allows you to choose the keywords that are most related to your application. This way, when someone does a search for your keywords, your paid ad may (emphasis on *may*) appear.

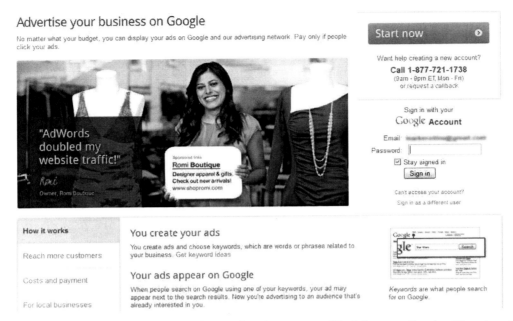

Figure 10-6. Google AdWords, a good way of getting more traffic right away (but it will cost you)

You might ask yourself if the extra exposure is worth it. Of course, it is possible to gain this type of exposure from social networks too.

Getting the Word Out on Your Social Networks

Remember when I said that you should develop Facebook friends and Twitter followers? I'm mentioning it again because it is so important. The ones who will want to know about your application are Android users, and it is really easy to inform them.

When it's time for you to send out the message to all your Facebook friends, use the method that I discussed earlier in Chapter 8, the one that I said not to abuse. The launch of your application is important, but other press releases, like "We achieved our thousandth download," not so much. You don't want to abuse your power in this way, or you will lose friends (when I say "friends," I mean the Facebook kind, but it might affect your personal friends as well).

While we're on the subject of Facebook, you should know that Facebook offers an advertising program based on click activity. You can create an advertisement for your application's page and even target this ad to certain people. Of course, this is about as risky as other paid search programs, such as AdWords. By the way, if you are offering a paid app, be sure to put the price of the application in the ad. You don't want users clicking it and then leaving after they find out there is a price!

Now is also a time where you can perfect that 140-character tweet and put out the official word that you have an application out. You don't want to post something like "My app is on the Android Market!" That is only helpful if your audience has been following the progress of your application. However, most Twitter users have hundreds, thousands, or (if they're celebrities) millions of followers, who can't keep track of their friend's tweets. You want something that is short and to the point—for example, "My Android app Baseball Card Organizer is now available on the Android Market for free."

I believe that I have said this before, but even though Twitter and Facebook are the most popular social networking sites, there are many more. Some of them are very specific, so you should check around to see what you can find that will suit the culture of your application.

The Season for Your Application

I discussed in Chapter 4 how important it is to set a launch date, and chances are, you are probably trying to get your app out by a certain time for a specific reason.

For example, if you have an application that helps people shop for gifts, you are probably going to want to get that out by Christmas. Considering the ways that stores prepare for the Christmas season, you might seriously think about having your app available after Halloween at the latest. Hopefully, you can get enough people who will use it by Black Friday (the day after Thanksgiving).

Since holidays are events that happen annually at the same time, they are quite easy to plan around, and there are times when your launch date will help that. For example, let's say that you have an exercise application, and you got it out the day after New Year's Day. Many people make new year's resolutions at this time, and a lot of them involve exercise. You could easily tailor your marketing campaign toward that. This could be addressed in your press release, on your site, and everywhere else.

In other words, you need to find what is going on, find a way that your application fits in, and show people that they need your application for this reason.

In a similar manner, you might be able to find a way for your application to piggyback on a current fad. *Piggyback marketing* is when you try to deliberately look like some other popular brand, while still maintaining your original idea.

If you want to see an example of piggybacking, go to the Young Adult section of a bookstore. For example, since Stephanie Meyer's *Twilight* series became popular, you can find plenty of books about vampires, and many of them have similar covers, fonts, and general looks. Chances are, those books were either trying to deliberately copy *Twilight*, or were written before *Twilight* and later released by publishing companies to capitalize on the Twilight fad.

In the same manner, you can dress up your application to match some fad that is rising. If the Super Bowl is coming up, you can emphasize your application's ability to keep track of teams.

■ **Note** When planning the timing of your release, remember to take into account beta testing time if you're going to include that for your app.

Considering a Temporary Giveaway

If you have a paid application, and are planning on making the bulk of your profits from that, you might want to consider suspending profits just so you can get some more copies of your application out there. What you want to do is offer your application for free, for a limited time only. By that time, word of mouth will spread that your application is great, and people will want to pay for what you have to offer.

Of course, this means that you need to get the word out that this application is only available for free for a limited time. That means you have write up another press release, and you will need to alter your description saying that it is free for a limited time. Tech blogs love to cover applications when they have a deal going on, so this can be a good course of action. Also remember to spread the word on your social networks and to others in your media circles about your deal.

One of the reasons for offering this deal is so you can end up in the Top New Free section on the Android Market. Who knows—if it does, you could end up in the Top New Paid section.

Also, there are web sites dedicated to free apps, such as Free Android App a Day (www.freeandroidappaday.com/). Getting your application on this or a similar site would be quite beneficial for anyone looking for free applications.

As I have said before, things have a way of selling better when they are free. Usually, although the temporary giveaway will cause you a loss initially, the end result will be a definite gain.

Getting Your Application a QR Code

Even if you have never used a QR (quick response) code before, you have probably at least seen one. They look like what you see in Figure 10-7.

Figure 10-7. You can go to the Android Market and download a QR code reader to scan this QR code. This QR Code will open up a URL for a web site that is worth visiting from time to time.

Hopefully, you have found a free application on the Android Market that will allow you to scan the QR code that you see here. You will find that it is a link to the URL for www.apress.com/. My Droid X phone allows me to easily share about Apress' web site via e-mail or SMS.

A QR code is a matrix bar code that is readable on QR readers, smartphones, and even webcams. The reason they are so popular is that they make it very simple for the user to gain information by scanning. There are many bar code scanner applications that are connected to the Android device's camera, and scanning these QR codes with one of these programs can open up access to a web site, and some of them will take the user straight to the Android market so the application can be downloaded in seconds.

Here's how you can get your own QR code for your application:

1. Go to the official Android Market web site at https://market.android.com/.
2. Use the search engine to find your application (see Figure 10-8).

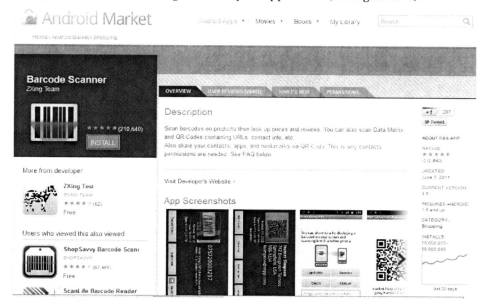

Figure 10-8. *An Android Market entry for Barcode Scanner. I highly recommend this application for scanning QR codes.*

3. Copy the URL for your application on the Android Market.
4. Go to the QR code generator at www.qrstuff.com/ (see Figure 10-9).

Figure 10-9. The QR Stuff web site; just one of many places to go for getting a QR code

5. On the QR Stuff page, select Website URL for the data type.

6. Paste the URL for your application in the Content section of the Android Market web site.

7. Select a foreground color.

8. Click Generate.

9. You will then see an image like the one in Figure 10-10.

Figure 10-10. *When you have your QR code, it should appear on the far right.*

10. You can then click "Download this image" to designate a place to store your QR code.

11. You can print out the code, send by e-mail, and choose from other options for the output type on the QR Stuff site.

Now you have a QR code that will come in handy for all kinds of occasions. For example, if you have a flier campaign, you can put the QR code on the corner. You can even make the fliers before the application is officially on the Android Market, and put a sticker with the QR code on them later.

This QR code is for anyone who has a bar code scanner on their Android-powered smartphone (or any other device for that matter). I have often seen QR codes and have scanned them just out of curiosity. Often, I have downloaded applications based on this discovery. When you can read QR codes, it's like you are living in a new sort of secret world.

You will also notice that in addition to making a QR code, the Kaywa QR code also makes a permalink that you can put in your web site's HTML code. All that is required is a quick copy-and-paste.

Yes, QR codes are a great gift to marketing. I once saw them being used on a roving billboard, and I thought it was a waste. If you are not familiar with roving billboards, they are these billboards on trucks that do nothing but drive around big cities, just so their sponsors can visually spread the word about their message. You can see a lot of them in downtown Las Vegas.

I remember being in Los Angeles and I saw a roving billboard for an application, and it had a QR code on it. I could not figure out why someone would put a QR code on a roving billboard. By the time I could whip out my phone and open the bar code–scanning app, the billboard had driven away. Too bad I can't remember the name of the application. That is a marketing failure! If it were on a stable billboard, that would be better; however, QR codes only work if you can focus on them with your bar code reader.

Breaking Out of the Box

In Chapter 2 I discussed Brostache, an application that puts a mustached mouth on the user. That application was featured prominently in a commercial for Geico about using one's smartphone for dumb things. In fact, it was the only application shown on that ad that was specifically named.

I would not be surprised if that whole "smartphone for dumb things" campaign was dreamed up so Brostache could be sold. Not that the application costs anything, but if you download it, you'll find that it really is an ad for Geico. You can even get your quote for car insurance right there.

Is this shameless marketing? I'll leave it up to you to decide. However, Brostache demonstrates how it's beneficial to think about different ways to promote your application. You might not be a big insurance company like Geico, but with your limited budget, you have to think of some way to get to your audience.

Summary

Now that you have an application that is out on the market, it is time to start thinking about what to do next. Ironically, the first step after your launch might be not marketing your application, as you might want to go into beta-testing mode. Beta testing will allow others to use your application, and you will find a lot of ways to improve after the beta testing is done.

Once you have your grand opening for your application, you can now spread the word. You can officially get your launch date press release out and spread the word on Twitter and Facebook as well.

Another important aspect of marketing your application is setting up a press room on your web site. This is a place where the media can go to download press kits, and see what others have written about your application. You also want to get a QR code for any print advertising for your application.

There are other ways of marketing your application, such as third-party press release distribution services, temporary giveaways, and paid searches, if you can afford them. It's also important to come up with creative ways of marketing your application, and ways that are appropriate for the season.

CHAPTER 11

Keep the Application Fires Burning

Now that you are past the launch date, I am going to talk about what you need to do if you want to keep going as an application developer. There are some products that have sold for decades and haven't changed their formula, such as Coca-Cola and Hershey's chocolate. (Coca-Cola actually tried to change its product's formula in 1985, which was a questionable business decision at best.)

This is not the case with applications. Applications need to change as the world around them changes. Also, technology becomes more and more advanced, which enables applications to add features that were not even dreamed of before.

Even if your product does not change, the marketing has to change. Coca-Cola and Hershey's have had several different marketing campaigns and slogans over the years as they change with the times. Your application is going to need different ways of marketing, because the old ways gradually lose their effect and get ignored by potential users.

How Will You Change?

It is smart to plan for certain changes in life. If you are expecting a new baby in your home, then you build a crib, prepare a diaper-changing station, and baby-proof your home. When the child grows up a little more, you prepare him or her for school, and hopefully you can prepare a college fund for when he or she leaves the house.

In the same way, you have to prepare your application for growth and change. As more and more users download a static or unchanging application, they will discover that it is limited, and they will begin to demand more. You will soon be receiving many e-mails, tweets, and Facebook wall posts requesting certain features that your application "obviously" should have. These requests may soon become demands.

If your competition makes an application that has what your users are demanding, then you can bet they will go to your competition, and quite possibly forget about your application. This could lead to a loss of downloads and a lot more bad reviews.

Take the time to sit down and think about what updates you will want to bring to your application in the future. I will discuss how to update your application later, but for now, think about these things as you consider the future of your application.

Following New Technology

Hopefully, you have subscribed to several tech and gadget blogs on an RSS feeder, just so you are in the know about what new technologies and developments are out there. If you discover a new technology that you can implement on your application, then you should be the first to have it. This is why you have to follow technological trends.

While you are trying to keep up with technology, be certain to be in the know as far as what is going on with Android. I discussed Android versions in Chapter 1, but subtle updates happen to Android on a monthly, if not daily, basis. There was a time when Android didn't have some of the features that it does now, including Voice Search, Voice Dial, and Bluetooth 2.1. Any advancement that happens to Android now could easily be seen as a standard feature in the near future.

Of course, some of the newest trends in technology tend to come out of the woodwork. I remember times when no one was on Facebook and Twitter, and then all of a sudden, it seemed like everyone was into social networking. Remember when only a few cell phones had cameras on them? Now, no cell phone manufacturer would release a mobile phone into the market without a camera. The same thing applies for Bluetooth and GPS. Word of mouth about tech advancements spreads very quickly.

Figuring Out the Season for Your Application

I'm sure you are quite familiar with Angry Birds, as it is very difficult to talk about successful applications without mentioning Rovio's hit mobile game. Rovio decided that Angry Birds was not enough for its fans, and created Angry Birds Seasons in the fall of 2010 (see Figure 11-1). Angry Birds Seasons has the same rules of the original game, with the slingshot and the attempt to destroy the evil green pigs who live in poorly built structures. The only difference is that the environments are seasonal. The first version was "Trick or Treat"; it was Halloween themed, and included pumpkins and black and orange props.

Figure 11-1. The game play of Rovio's Angry Birds Seasons is just like the very popular Angry Birds, but the visuals are made for specific seasons.

Since the first Angry Birds Seasons was a hit, Rovio followed it up with an update called "Seasons Greedings," which used a Christmas holiday theme. In 2011, Rovio improved Seasons with "Hogs and Kisses" (Valentine's Day themed), "Go Green Get Lucky" (St. Patrick's Day themed), and "Easter Eggs" (I probably don't need to tell you the theme of that). Rovio released a summer-themed Angry Birds Seasons ("Summer Pignic"), and even released another version of Angry Birds, known as Angry Birds Rio. This game is a movie tie-in of a computer-animated movie about birds.

Rovio realized that it needed to change Angry Birds, but it decided not to change the game play itself (a decision I agree with). Instead, Rovio created new versions of the old game, and gave them new themes, anticipating the changing of seasons. It also planned for the release of *Rio*, and the movie's success helped promote the game.

In the same manner, you need to update your application with the changing of the seasons. As I discussed in the last chapter about your launch date, every month seems to have a holiday or theme associated with it, and you can make your app more desirable by updating it to account for this.

Planning Around the Holidays and Seasons

When I worked at a retail store, we had sections of the store that were seasonal, and planned for consumers' needs during certain times of the year.

In February, it was Valentine's Day, and the seasonal aisles were decorated with red, pink, and white cards and candy. It then shifted to Easter, where the candy was in different packaging with baskets and plastic grass. During summertime, these aisles were filled with squirt guns, portable swimming pools, kites, and other outdoor toys. Then came the back-to-school time in August and September, and these aisles were filled with pencils, paper, and other school supplies. In October, it was candy again, with spooky Halloween costumes and paraphernalia thrown in. I'll leave you to imagine what was in the aisles in November and December, in anticipation of Christmas.

The reason that I bring up the subject of the seasonal aisles is that it is easy to plan what items will sell at these given times. Holidays are events that you can plan around. And just as important as the holidays are people's general moods during these time.

In January, people are all about New Year's resolutions and bettering themselves, so this is a good time to sell health and productivity applications. Valentine's Day is in February, a time when people tend to think of love and relationships, so this would be a good time to market an application related to these. Any application related to vacation planning would probably sell well in the summer. By now, you should be able to see a pattern forming.

Once you've figured out the purpose of your application, you should be able to figure out what times of the year it will sell the best. It might be a certain holiday, or just some time of the year when people will be thinking about doing a certain thing that your application can help them with. Plan for this time and get the word out to your contacts at this time, and you will be able to sell more than you normally would.

Figuring Out Your Peak Period

In the same way, your application may have a peak period during which it sells the most, and may hardly have any downloads at other times.

For example, if you create an application that follows the NCAA games, you are going to see an increase during March Madness, and then nothing until next basketball season.

▪ **Note** If you can create an application that follows the basketball season, it isn't too difficult to create an application that follows the baseball, football, and/or hockey seasons as well. Doing so could allow you to capitalize on multiple peak periods.

Some applications, such as tax preparation apps, have longer peak times. With this type of app, chances are you will see a lot of downloads between January and April, as people prepare for the income tax deadline, but only a few downloads by procrastinators in May. Then your application could be completely forgotten during summer or fall.

If you can make a living on one application's peak period, then you should consider yourself quite lucky. However, a better strategy is to have many applications going at once, focus on each one during its peak season, and use the non-peak off-season to prepare for updates for next year.

How to Update Your Android Application

In this section, I am going to assume that you have discovered a way to improve your application, and you have gone into your application and altered the code significantly enough that you can justify an official update of your application. You may have also discovered a bug in the application that you have finally figured out how to fix. This section will describe how you can update your application using Eclipse and the Android Market publisher site.

After you have made all the updates to your application, make certain that it runs without errors. I recommend *regression testing* to uncover new errors that appear after you change it, not to mention a barrage of tests to ensure error-free running. You should also run it on an emulator or Android device to make certain that your new features run exactly as planned.

Open up your application on Eclipse. Before you put your update on the Android Market, you have to update your `AndroidManifest.xml` file in your Android program. When you upload your APK to the Android Market, it automatically defaults to this underneath the package prompt in the first few lines of the `AndroidManifest`:

```
android: versionCode = "1"
android: versionName = "1.0"
```

You will want to change the `android: versionCode` to 2, and you can change the `android: versionName` to whatever you want. You probably shouldn't change the version name to 2.0 unless this is a major update of some type. I will leave you to decide what that is. To put it in perspective, I made a few updates on my first application after it was out on the market for a few days. I figured that a version name of 1.1 was appropriate (see Figure 11-2).

Figure 11-2. *The typical Android manifest for a program on Eclipse. Note the version code and version name, which will need to be changed for an update.*

With Eclipse already open, you will need to digitally sign your application again, like you did before when you first submitted to the Android Market.

Right-click the top of the application in Package Explorer, and select Android Tools and Export Signed Application Package. You should see a window like in Figure 11-3.

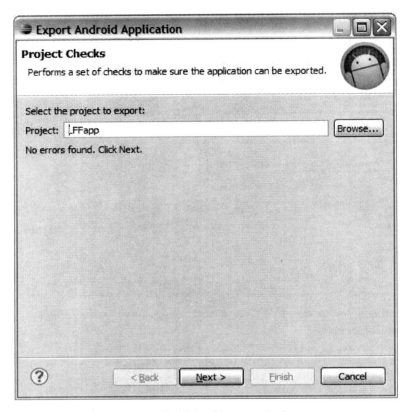

Figure 11-3. The Export Android Application window

Go ahead and select your project. If it's not there by default, select the proper project and click Next. You should see a window like in Figure 11-4.

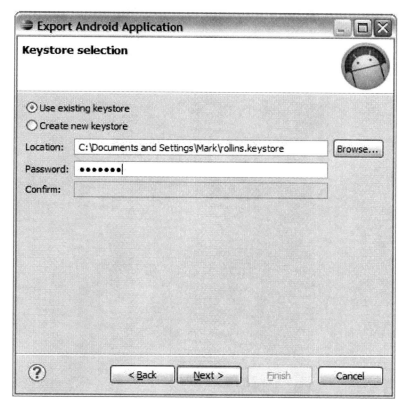

Figure 11-4. The "Keystore selection" screen of the Export Android Application dialog

From here, it will default to "Use existing keystore," and it should default to where you put your keystore the first time. If it doesn't, click the Browse button and find the directory where you put the keystore that you wish to use. Enter the password and confirm it, and then click Next. You will then see a window like in Figure 11-5.

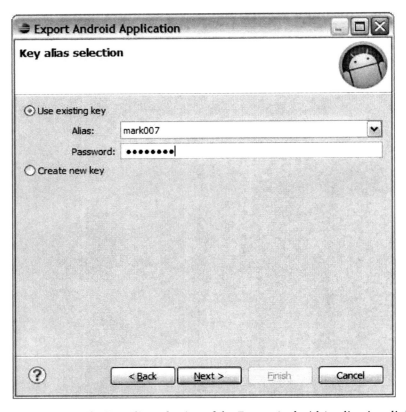

Figure 11-5. The Key Alias selection of the Export Android Application dialog

If you input your password correctly, you will get a screen like in Figure 11-6, with your alias appearing by default. If you didn't input it correctly, you'll get a message that says, "Keystore was tampered with or password was incorrect." If you run into this problem, just click Back, and try entering your password again.

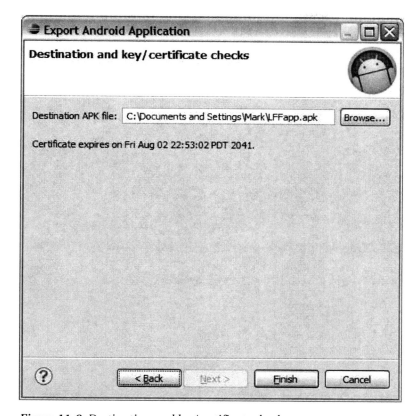

Figure 11-6. *Destination and key/certificate checks*

According to the official Android Market publishing site, at http://developer.android.com/guide/publishing/publishing.html, "The package name must be the same as the existing version and the .apk file must be signed with the same private key. If the package name and signing certificate do *not* match those of the existing version, Market will consider it a new application, publish it as such, and will not offer it to existing users as an update." Consider this package name your unique ID on the market.

This means that you want to make your APK file and your file name the same, so you should go into your file manager and save your old APK file with a different name, such as *file name* Vers 1, just so you have the original version, in case you need it again. In fact, I usually copy the entire directory, and I recommend zipping it as an archive. Just go to your file manager, right-click the folder, and click Send To ➤ "Compressed (zipped) folder."

Once you have the new destination APK file, go ahead and click the Finish button.

Now you will need to go to the Android Market and officially put out the new version of your application. Open your browser to the Android Market at http://market.android.com/publish. Log in with the username and password that you set up when you originally published your application, as shown in Figure 11-7.

Figure 11-7. *The opening page of the Android Market publishing site*

After you have finished logging in, you will see an "All Android Market listings" page, like one shown in Figure 11-8.

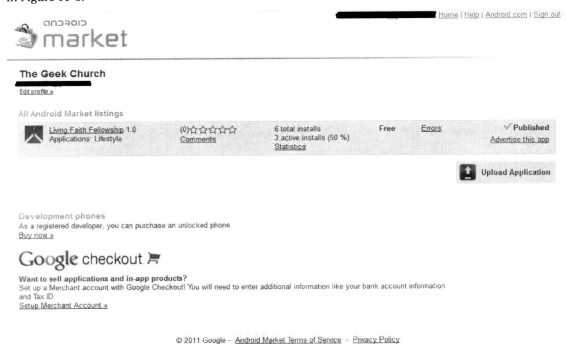

Figure 11-8. *The "All Android Market listings" page will have a list of all of the applications you have on the Android Market.*

Select the app to be updated. Click "APK files" and you will see a screen like in Figure 11-9.

Figure 11-9. The screen for editing your application

Click Unpublish. This will take your application off the market until you put it back on again. The Unpublish button will change to read "Publish," as shown in Figure 11-10.

Figure 11-10. Unpublishing your application on the Android Market publishing site

You will need to upload the new APK, so click Upload APK. You should see a window like Figure 11-11.

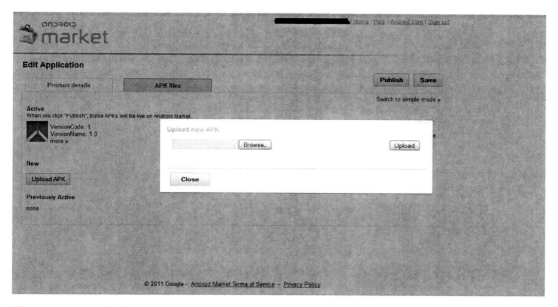

Figure 11-11. *Uploading the new APK*

Browse to wherever you saved your new APK, and click Upload. You will see a screen like the one shown in Figure 11-12.

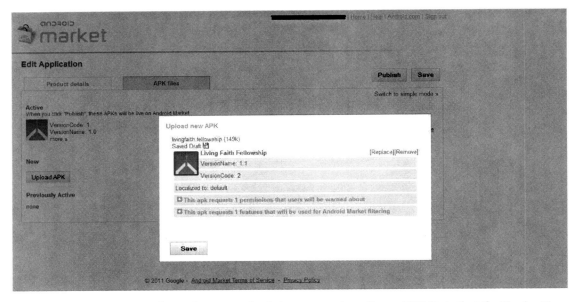

Figure 11-12. What you will see after you upload the new version of your APK. Note that the VersionName and VersionCode have changed.

If your application has changed as far as user permissions go, you will get a warning, as shown in Figure 11-12. Click Save, and you will see a screen like Figure 11-13.

Figure 11-13. What you will see after you update your APK

Your application cannot handle two versions of the same APK, so it will ask you to deactivate one of them. Go ahead and deactivate the old version, and activate the new. Click Save and then Publish.

If you've made any significant changes, you should probably open the program to the editing screen and make a note of whatever changes you've made. These will show up in the official Android Market entry. To do this, click the "Product details" tab, and enter a description of your changes in the Recent Changes text box, as shown in Figure 11-14.

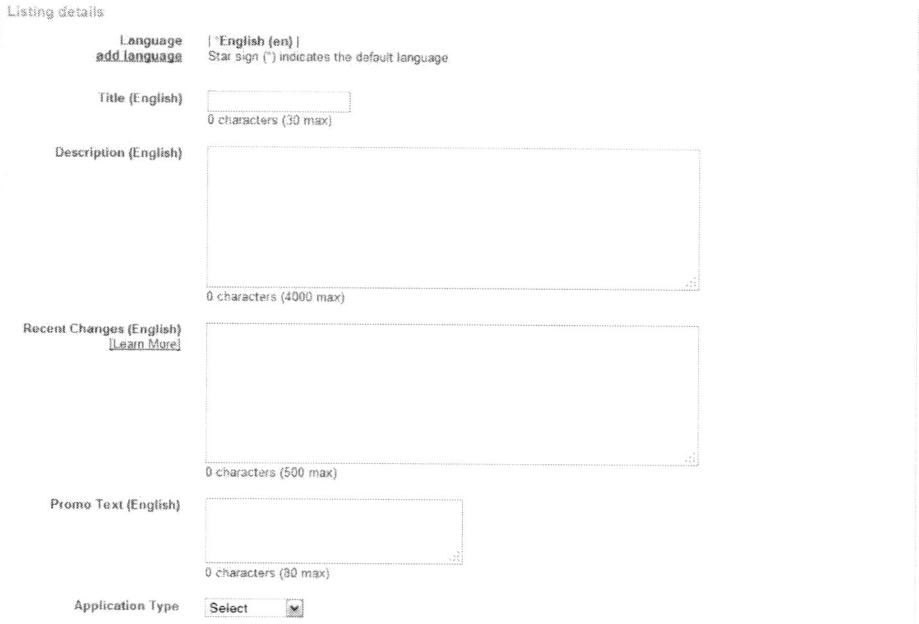

Listing details

Language add language	| *English (en) | Star sign (*) indicates the default language
Title (English)	_____ 0 characters (30 max)
Description (English)	 0 characters (4000 max)
Recent Changes (English) [Learn More]	 0 characters (500 max)
Promo Text (English)	 0 characters (80 max)
Application Type	Select

Figure 11-14. *Noting the recent changes to your updated application*

Okay, now that you have completed your first Android update, do not let it be your last. You are going to have to keep doing more and more updates to keep up with consumers' needs. If you do an update that is a complete renovation of your application, this should be considered a new version.

▪ **Tip** For some reason, new versions that end in zero get a lot of attention. Mozilla recently took advantage of this, moving Firefox rapidly to 5.0 and then 6.0. ^). You should consider doing the same with your application.

When you put version 2.0 on the market, be certain that all your media contacts and social networks are informed of this. It is a big deal! The same goes for your 3.0, 4.0, and so on.

Now that you are an application developer, it is necessary to do maintenance of more than just your applications to keep your career alive and fruitful. You are also going to need to change your marketing practices from time to time, and make new announcements for each improvement (possibly even press releases).

At some point in the life of your application, maintenance begins to take precedence over creation. This is not to say that you should stop being creative when you have a moneymaking application. If anything, you should always be looking to improve on what you have made.

One way of finding out how you can improve is by looking at your feedback via e-mail or social networking sites. You will find out real fast, often through negative criticism, what your application needs or does not need.

Using Google Statistics

If you look at Figure 9-15, you will see a link on Android Market called Statistics.

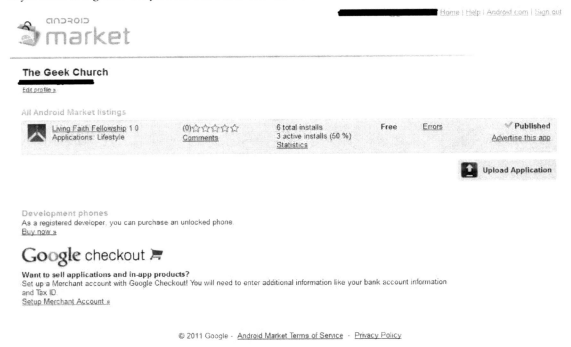

Figure 11-15. *The Statistics area can give you vital information about how your application is selling.*

The Statistics area shows a lot of useful information, including a graph of total active installs of your app. You will also see attributes breakdown of platform versions in pie chart form, which will show what versions of Android your users are using. It will also show you a pie chart of what specific devices are being used, and what countries and languages your application is being downloaded in.

You can use this information to figure out important information about how your application is progressing. For example, you may notice that your application is not being downloaded on certain models of Android phones. Uh-oh! Does that mean that your application is having problems downloading on that particular type of Android phone? That is most certainly worth looking into. Hopefully, you can use the data to discover problems before your users start complaining about them in the form of negative reviews.

In addition to monitoring how your application is doing on the market, there are other ways you can gain useful knowledge out in the field.

Attending Conferences

As a reporter for the tech and gadget scene, I find it extremely valuable to attend tech conferences. There are quite a few that happen throughout the year, and some of them are annual events.

If you go online and run a search for "Android Developers Conferences," you will find more than a few. There are also local Java developer conferences across the country. You don't want to go to just any tech or gadget conference, of course. You should focus on the ones that are designed specifically for application developers who deal with Android; these are terrific places to showcase your product.

If you're planning to attend a particular conference, try to make the arrangements several months in advance, which will allow you time to reserve some space on the conference floor and build a booth with your company logo, and thus attract some attention. Keep in mind, however, that these conferences can be expensive. If you are a new company without a lot of cash for the conference, you will probably find yourself placed on the sidelines with other startup companies. As a result, you will be eclipsed by booths from bigger companies.

In the case of CES (Consumer Electronics Show), I usually don't see many application developers with booths of their own, unless they are tied to some other product. For example, if a company is making an electronic device, sometimes they'll have an application specifically designed for the device.

CES is a consumer electronics expo, as opposed to a developer-specific expo, so it might not be the best place to put your application on display. I still recommend attending the conference because companies have their new products prominently on display. As a developer, you want to know about what new technology is coming out, and CES is often the place where electronics companies show what they intend to have out for the year.

Big industry conferences like CES and CTIA (Cellular Telecommunications Industry Association, which has two shows, in spring and fall) often have other ways that exhibitors can show off their products apart from the show floor. There are often press-only events, such as ShowStoppers and Pepcom, that are designed so companies can introduce their products to the media. As a reporter, I often prefer these other smaller shows as opposed to the huge displays at these conferences. These smaller shows often have good food and not as much of a crowd, so it is easier to talk to the people that I need to talk to.

I have seen some application developers at conferences who see my press pass and ask for a moment of my time so they can talk about their product. I would imagine that they probably couldn't afford a booth or a press show. This approach can work if you are willing to come to the media contact, instead of letting them come to you. I know that I have written a lot of great articles simply because someone has come up to me and asked, "Hey, can I show you what my company is doing?"

Even though many big companies get a big spotlight at these tech shows, a simple tech blogger like me likes to walk around conferences looking for something new. I love it when I walk past a booth and the person there greets me as if he or she was expecting me. I then tell them who I am and who I write for, and they tell me about their product. This way, the approach is personal.

I also like to take the occasional swag (stuff we all get). Many companies give out some items at their booths with their logo on it. These items can range from T-shirts, to keychains, to candy, to flashlights, and they're designed so that you have a physical object to remember the company that you visited.

If the product interests me and I can write an article about it, I will get the information that I need. Usually, the company has a press kit in the form of a CD-ROM or a thumb drive that contains all the images, logos, information, and everything else that should be contained in a press kit. I usually take a business card to make certain that I can get more information later, if I need it.

In short, I highly recommend setting up time at a tech convention in order to get the word out about your application once it is readily available on the Android Market. When you find these conferences, make certain that you register properly, and be in communication with the conference/convention center about what you will need to set up.

If you don't have the money for a booth or table, at least make up some press kits in CD-ROM or thumb-drive form. Talk to as many people as you can, especially if they are in the media, and start a collection of business cards. Make certain to give out some of your own as well. By the time the convention is over, you will have begun to create some good word of mouth about your application. Conferences like AnDevCon are made for Android Developers, and Google has one of its own called Google I/O every year as well.

The Price

By now your application is out on the market, and has a price, even if that price is "free." You might be using that suggestion in Chapter 6 about having a paid version and a free version.

Prices are not set in stone and can be changed. If you want to leave your free version without updating it, and always have it be that purposely pale shadow of the paid version, that is up to you. However, I recommend a few updates of the free one, just so you can always get the potential paying audience. In other words, don't always put all your good eggs in just one basket.

Since the price can be changed, you might want to try an experiment of raising or lowering your application's price, just to see how your users react. One developer told me that he had a $0.99 application, and he upped the price from $0.99 to $1.99 for a week, then $2.99, then $3.99. What he learned was that he had 100 sales in a week at $0.99, and then he had about 45 sales at $1.99. He made less overall, but it was close. Then he upped the price of the application to $2.99 and he still had 45 sales per week, which comes out to roughly 145 percent of the $0.99 app revenue. That's not bad.

When to Do a Price Increase

No consumer likes it when inflation occurs. I would like to say that price increases are a necessary evil, and only in place because prices of other things increase, but I would be lying. The fact is, a price increase is very good for you, and if you are pouring a lot into your business, you have to have price increases to justify staying in business. Price increases happen all the time in the business world, and they should happen to you, if you need them.

So when do you do price increases? If your product is at the peak period discussed earlier, this is the best time to get the highest price you can for it. In fact, you might want run a "special" on your application, offering it for a reduced price during part of the peak, and then run it at the regular price for the remainder of the peak. If your application has a season, as discussed earlier in this chapter, this is also a good time for a price increase.

How much you want to increase your price is up to you, but if an increase is too great, then you will have to be prepared for a barrage of criticism. Don't be surprised if you get a lot of people who divvy out the one-star reviews because they don't want to pay a high price.

When to Do a Price Decrease

Occasionally, you will discover that your application isn't working out the way you expected it to. You may discover that there have been very few downloads.

In that case, the only way to possibly increase sales is to mark it down, possibly to permanently free. In Chapter 4, I talked about how some applications are stars, some are cash cows, some are problem children, and some are dogs. If you have a problem child, then you may need bring it down to free just so you can get some advertising profit off it, or else it will become a dog. If the application is so totally hopeless, it might be worth taking it off the market entirely just so it doesn't demean you or your company by being attached to you.

You may have a simple problem child that just needs to be improved before the real sales on it begin. If so, I recommend a temporary price decrease on the current version. You will have to get the word out through your media outlets, social networks, and other venues that you are doing this, of course.

I have discovered that news of a price reduction can often lead to rumors about the demise of a product. For example, when Nintendo reduced the price of the GameCube to $99, it looked pretty bad for the company. As it turns out, it was a way to compete with Sony and Microsoft until the Wii could be launched. Then the Wii became the great competitor.

In other words, if you spread the word about a price reduction on your application, don't be surprised if someone else spreads word saying that your application is dying. This is the time when you can prove them wrong by writing an updated version.

You might want to release the updated version during the price decrease. This way, Android users discover something worthwhile at a lower price. Then, by the time the application goes back to the regular price, people will be more willing to pay the regular price.

Summary

This concludes the discussion on marketing your Android application. You should still read the next chapter, which will teach a lot about programming with Android.

If you're already a programming expert, then let me give you the last bit of advice that I can: keep moving forward when it comes to your applications. If you want to start a career as a developer, then you are going to have to continually create new applications as well as improve upon the older ones. That can be a difficult juggling act.

I am not that experienced of a developer, but speaking as a writer, I know how hard it is to begin something new. Oftentimes, you have to make the time to start the new thing, and it is often easier just to perpetuate the old, even though the old can be out of date. I'm sure that you have discovered that there are a lot of applications and other businesses that are outmoded and maybe even obsolete, but people still maintain them out of a weird sense of tradition. Don't let that happen to your applications. If an application can be improved, try it. If it can't be improved, and you have tried, then let it go and try something else.

The important thing is that you keep on trying, keep on improving, and keep moving forward in your career. This is a time when you want to hold on to milestones such as your thousandth or millionth download. Keep those milestones around not so you can brag, but so you can keep track of your progress.

Keep making progress in your programming as well. Programming is something that is tough to learn at first. The more you do it, the easier it becomes, but it really never becomes easy if you are always trying to innovate.

If you can find help programming, don't be afraid to ask for it, but don't ask for it too much. There have been times that I have been stuck, and I asked for help, only to discover that had I given the problem a few more hours, I probably could have stumbled onto the solution myself.

The only reason why I have succeeded in programming is because I had help. I know some people who are like gurus of programming. That is, they have some odd instinct that allows them to just look at a problem and see a solution. Chances are, that solution just comes to them because they have had a similar problem that they worked out in the past.

Even programming gurus get stuck at times, and encounter things that are difficult, especially if they are trying to do something new. I guarantee you that the more original your idea for your application, the harder it will be to implement. Hopefully it will be easy to market an application that solves a specific and unique problem, but don't count on it!

Chances are, what you are doing on your application has probably been done before, and you can do a keyword search on Google to discover how to solve the problem. Simple things like buttons and interfaces have much written on them online.

I have found that programming applications is fun because of the joy of creation. The more original your idea is, the more joy it brings, but the harder it is to bring it about.

I wish you the best on your applications, and hope that you can really change the market itself. Enjoy bringing about change, and don't quit unless you can afford to.

CHAPTER 12

Programming in Android with the Eclipse IDE

This chapter is all about how to program with the Eclipse IDE, which is a great tool to use when creating an Android application. I already talked in Chapter 1 about how to set up the Eclipse IDE with the Java JDK and the Android SDK.

This chapter is for those Android developers who have never programmed before. You will discover how Java, Android's main programming language, works, and there is an application that you can write at the end. The purpose of this chapter is to make you as an Android developer understand the programming commitment that must be made in order to put out an application that will succeed in the crowded market. I hope that it helps you figure out how long it will take to write your application so that you can create a marketing plan around its creation.

If you want to learn about Android programming in greater detail, I highly recommend reading *Android Apps for Absolute Beginners* (Apress, 2010), by Wallace Jackson, a programming master whose book helped me out quite a bit.

Setting Up the Eclipse IDE to Work with the Android SDK

Go ahead and open up the Eclipse IDE. If you like, you can start a new workspace, or simply use the one that you may have been working with before. Once you select your workspace, you should see a screen like Figure 12-1.

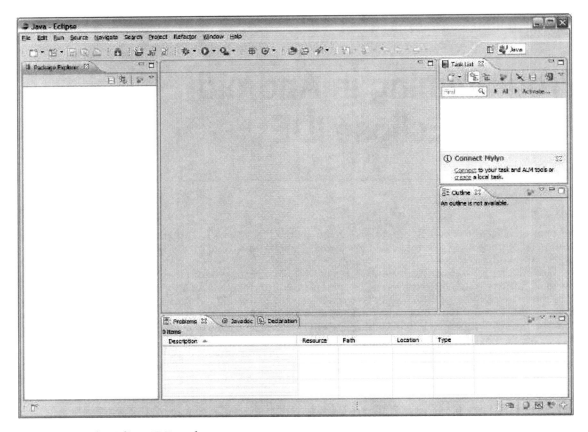

Figure 12-1. The Eclipse IDE workspace

The panel on the left is known as Package Explorer, which is a place for the folder hierarchy. The Task List and Outline panels on the right will also help you with your application. The panel at the bottom right is very helpful as well, as it will give you important information during various stages of your programming. The center panel (blank in Figure 12-1) is the editor, which is where you will be inputting your code.

If you are using a new workspace, then you are going to need to set up your project to work with the Android SDK. You will need to select Windows and then Preferences. You will see a window like Figure 12-2.

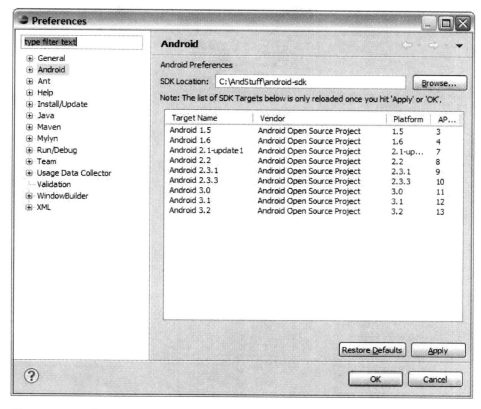

Figure 12-2. What you will see when you set up your preferences in the Eclipse IDE

In the Preferences window, you will see a list on the left. Select the Android option, as shown in Figure 12-2.

You will see a tab marked "SDK location." Click Browse and find the directory where you put the Android SDK. You should see the area under the "SDK location" tab fill with information, as in Figure 12-2. Click Apply, and you can have a build target for when you create an Android project.

Starting a New Android Project

Now it is time to start a new Android application. From the toolbar, select File ➤ New ➤ Android Project. You should see a menu like in Figure 12-3. The versions of Android may be different, depending on the versions that you set up earlier.

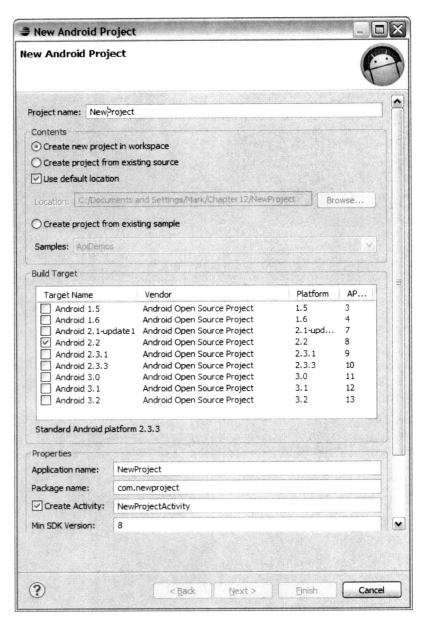

Figure 12-3. Starting a new project for Android on Eclipse will reveal this window.

Figure 12-3 has to be filled out in a certain way, and I will go through the steps.

We'll start with the obvious, the project name. Whatever you type into the "Project name" field will be the name of the file that it will be in your workspace file directory. Spaces are not supported in Java names, so if the name of your project is a few words, you have to run them together. For example, Brand New Project would have to become BrandNewProject. The project name does not have to be the name of your application, as you learned in Chapter 9 when you created an APK file.

As for the Contents section, you have many options. If you select "Create new project in workspace," this creates an original Android project. If your project is similar to one that already exists, such as an application that you created before, you can select your project from some other source in your directory. You can also select from a default location, which automatically selects from the workspace that is currently being used.

You can even "borrow" from some existing sample. For example, you can take from some of the SDK samples, provided they give you license. I found that I was able to incorporate a sample file known as Notepad into my Android application, and all that was required was that I include a copy of the license in the Android code. If you would like to use the code in these samples, check to see if they will give you license, and what steps you will need to follow to get it. These samples are found in the Android SDK file under the appropriately named folder samples.

These samples are separated into files for different versions of Android, so you will have to use the proper version for the proper sample. These samples range from simple games like Lunar Lander to interesting applications like Notepad.

In the Build Target section, select the version of Android you want to use for your Android project. You have hopefully loaded it up properly. Remember that if you want more people to download your application, you are going to have to use a lower version of Android. I recommend version 1.6, which will enable all the Boost Mobile users as well as the more advanced Android crowd.

In the Properties section, you enter the application name, which Eclipse will use to set up the framework for your application. It is precisely what shows in the application's title bar as the app runs. So whatever you want on your title bar, put here; this *can* have spaces and punctuation.

The package name is what needs to be used for your Java package. It is the container that holds all of the Java code that the application uses. Java packages are separated by periods, to indicate the hierarchy. A Java package starts with the highest-level domain name of the organization, with all subdomains listed in reverse order. This could be anything; in this example I chose new.project.

You can leave the Create Activity box selected. This Java activity class is a collection of code that controls your user interface.

The Min SDK Version field is where you declare the version of Android yet again; here it has to match. I believe it defaults to the same build target:

- 3 = Android 1.5

- 4 = Android 1.6

- 5 = Android 2.0

- 6 = Android 2.0.1

- 7 = Android 2.1 update 1

- 8 = Android 2.2

- 9 = Android 2.3.1

- 10 = Android 2.3.3

- 11 = Android 3.0

- 12 = Android 3.1

- 13 = Android 3.2

There might be other versions out by the time you are reading this. For now, click Finish and that is all.

What You Will Notice About Your Android Project Structure

One of the things that you will notice about Eclipse is how it does a lot of autogeneration. Package Explorer generates some interesting default folders, as shown on the left side of Figure 12-4.

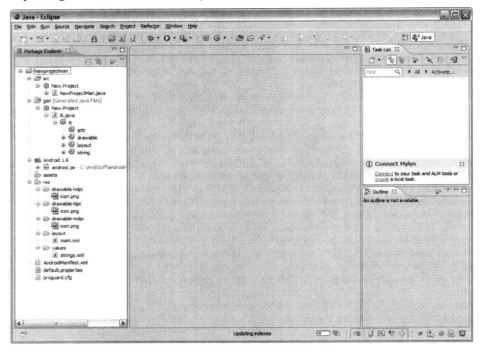

Figure 12-4. *After you start up a new Android project, you will see a new file directory in Package Explorer.*

You should know that these are not the only types of folders that one can have on an Android project. I guarantee you that you will want to make new ones. The following list briefly describes what these folders and files are for:

- src: This is the source folder. You will quickly notice that whatever you choose as the package name will be in the file. This contains the Java code that drives an application.

- gen: This contains Java files generated by ADT. The gen folder contains items generated from the res directory. Generally, it is recommended not to mess with this manually, as it might not compile by itself.

- `android.jar`: As you can tell, this matches your build target. It is an item in Eclipse presented through ADT.

- `assets`: This folder is by default empty, but it is made to store raw asset files. Raw assets (for example, a SQLite database) could be required to get your application to work.

- `res`: This stands for *resources,* and there are a lot of important files here. There are many subdirectories, and most of them are in XML files, including the following:

    - `anim/` for animations

    - `color/` for a list of colors

    - `drawable/` for bitmap files (I will explain the `hdpi`, `mdpi`, and `ldpi` files later)

    - `layout/` for a user interface layout

    - `menu/` for application menus

    - `raw/` for arbitrary files in their raw form

    - `values/` for simple values, including resource arrays, colors, dimensions, strings, and styles

- `AndroidManifest.xml`: This is the first file that an Android application will seek out. It is always located in the directory structure so it is easy to find. Here are some of the things that it contains:

    - References to the Java code that you will write for your application so the code can be both found and run.

    - Definitions of permissions for application security and for talking with other Android applications.

    - Definitions of the components of the Android application, including when they can be launched.

    - Declaration of the minimum level of Android operating system version support.

- `default.properties`: This is a file used with both Eclipse and ADT, and it contains the project settings. Like the gen file, it should not be tampered with manually.

- `proguard.cfg`: This is automatically generated in the root directory of the project. According to the Android Developers site, the ProGuard tool "shrinks, optimizes, and obfuscates your code by removing unused code and renaming classes, fields, and methods with semantically obscure names."

Let's look at what is in the files. At any given time, we can edit what is in the folders in three ways:

- Double-clicking the file

- Right-clicking the file and clicking Open

- Selecting the file and clicking F3

This will open up the file in the editor, and you can make changes accordingly.

Uploading the Icon and Background for Your Android Application

By now, you should have decided what type of icon you want, as well as the background for your application. These are important elements of your style, which I discussed in Chapter 3.

You will notice that the `drawable` folder in the `res` folder of Package Explorer has three folders: `hdpi`, `mdpi`, and `ldpi`. You will also notice that each of them has a file of the same name, `icon.png`. `icon.png` is set up for different types of bitmap images. These are the required measurements for the icon and background, in pixels:

- *hdpi* is for high-density DPI screen images. The icon must be 72×72 pixels, and the background must be 800×480 pixels.

- *mdpi* is for medium-density DPI screen images. The icon must be 48×48 pixels, and the background must be 320×480 pixels.

- *ldpi* is for low-density DPI screen images. The icon must be 32×32 pixels, and the background 320×420 pixels.

It is important that your icon and background conform to these dimensions, as Android is set up for them for very specific instances. For example, shifting your application from portrait to landscape mode will look much better if your background is presented correctly.

How to Replace the Default icon.png File

Note that each of the `drawable` folders in Figure 12-4 has a specific image file known as `icon.png`, which is the bitmap for the icon. What you want to do is replace that default icon, which is nothing more than the Android logo in its default state, as shown in Figure 12-5.

Figure 12-5. *The default Android icon, which automatically appears when you create an Android application*

Here are some steps you can follow to change the default icon to one that you have designed:

1. You should get the graphics that you want for your icon, and save it in PNG format if it is not already. You can easily convert your image from its current file type by opening up Microsoft Windows' default Paint program and saving the image in PNG format.

2. You will need to crop the PNG image so that it's square—preferably 200×200 pixels (it can be larger, provided the length equals the width). This can be accomplished in Microsoft Office Picture Manager by selecting the image,

selecting Picture from the top menu, and then selecting Crop. The Crop tool can make your image square; you can see the exact numbers of pixels in your image on the right, in the "Picture dimensions" section (see Figure 12-6).

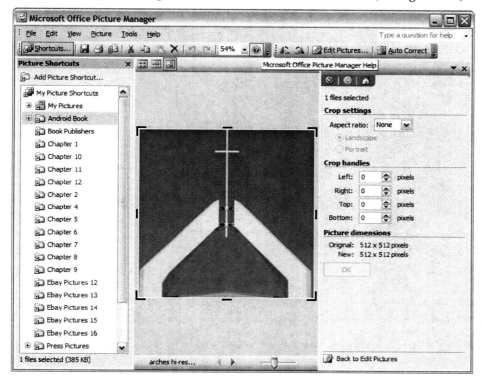

Figure 12-6. *Using Microsoft Office Picture Manager is one way of turning your graphic for your icon into a perfect square.*

3. You can use the Resize tool (also a selectable from the picture menu bar) to bring your image to the appropriate size (see Figure 12-7). Keep in mind that Picture Manager's resizing tool can distort things, so you might want to try Photoshop or other tools that can resize an image.

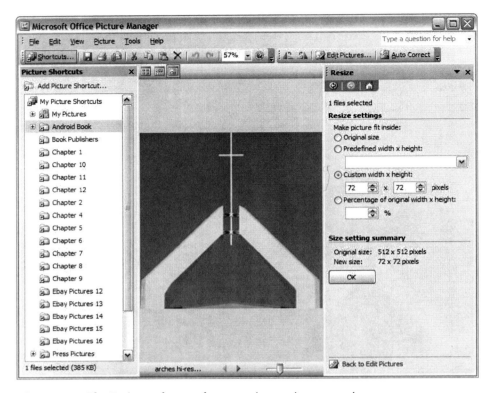

Figure 12-7. *The Resize tool can reduce your icon to its proper size.*

4. Resize your icon to 72×72 for the hdpi version and click OK. Click Save As from the top menu. Go to the directory where you saved your workspace, and click the res folder and then drawable-hdpi. Save the file as icon.png. It will ask you if you want to overwrite, so click Yes. See Figure 12-8.

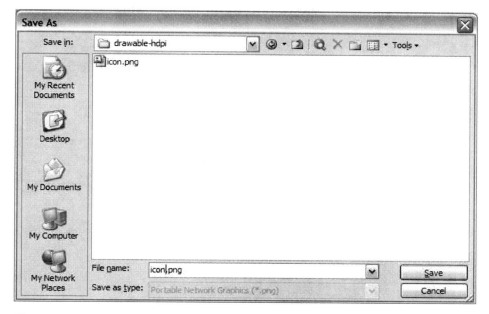

Figure 12-8. *Saving your icon as an icon.png file (in the proper format) will ensure that it will show up in your application.*

5. Go back to your original image (preferably 200×200), resize it to 48×48 for the mdpi file, and Click OK. Click Save As from the top menu.

6. Go to the directory where you saved your workspace, and click the res folder and then drawable-mdpi. Save the file as icon.png. It will ask you if you want to overwrite, so click Yes.

7. Repeat Steps 5 and 6 for your icon, this time for ldpi; the dimensions need to be 32×32.

You now have your icon for all three different screen resolutions.

How to Set a Background

If you do not set a background for your application, it will appear as a black, blank screen, as shown in Figure 12-9. Since that is a little boring, you should make one of your own, one that is consistent with your style.

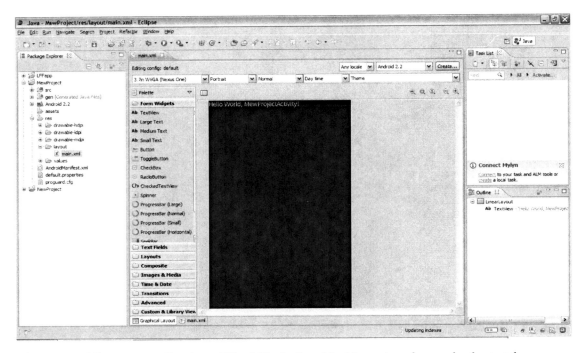

Figure 12-9. What your application will look like in Graphical Layout mode, sans background

Similar to the steps for the icon, you will need to create a `background.png` file for the `hdpi`, `mdpi`, and `ldpi` files. The one for `hdpi` has to be 800×480 pixels, the one for `mdpi` has to be 320×480 pixels, and the one for `ldpi` must be 320×420 pixels. Save them under the same name (`background.png`) in the same manner that you saved the `icon.png` file.

Sadly, Android does not automatically set the background, but you can use a simple line of code to do it yourself in `main.xml`:

```
android:background="@drawable/background
```

Perfect. It has gone from ugly black to customized! If you want to see what it looks like, feel free to jump ahead and check out Figure 12-17.

Understanding Java SE

The Android development environment is essentially a combination of Java and XML. The Android SDK includes a runtime that translates the Java and XML code into a language that the operating system and the individual device can understand.

XML stands for eXtensible Markup Language, and it is very similar to the HTML (HyperText Markup Language) that is used for web site design. In fact, HTML is a subset or implementation of XML. XML is designed to structure data for items that require a predefined data structure, and to define constructs so that the user does not need to create them in more complex Java code. If you have done any work in HTML, you will see a familiar sight in XML, known as *tags*. These tags are bracketed by < and > characters.

Android works with Java Standard Edition, or Java SE. Java SE was created by Oracle, and is much more powerful than Java Micro Edition (Java ME), which is on most mobile phones. What you need to know about Java is that it is an object-oriented programming (OOP) language. What you need to know about OOP is that it uses modular, self-contained constructs known as *objects*. Objects, like all programming constructs, are merely abstractions intended to help programmers model certain aspects of the real world in terms of logic and math.

Objects

If you need an example of an object in programming, just look around you for physical objects around the room. Right now, I am sitting in a coffee shop and I am trying to figure out the objects as a computer program would see them. A computer doesn't necessarily know the importance of any given object, unless it is properly defined. To define these objects around me, I am going to pretend that I am receiving a call from my cell phone, and the person on the other end wants me to describe the room around me. How I define it is really up to me, as long as it makes sense to the person on the other end.

I see a chair, and it is made of wood, with four legs, and let's say that it is 3 feet (36 inches) tall. In front of me is a table, and it is made of metal. Let's say the table is 37 inches tall, and only has one leg (due to a wide base on the bottom).

Here is my formula for a chair:

```
class Chair {
int legs = 4;
int height = 36;
String material = "Wood";
}
```

Here is a formula for a table:

```
class Table {
int legs = 1;
int height = 37;
String material = "Metal";
}
```

In the cases above, the blueprint is set with the single word class, and then the object. Within the curly brackets ({ and }) are the variables that hold the states of the objects. *States* are the characteristics of the objects. In terms of grammatical parts of speech, think of the objects as the nouns and the characteristics as the adjectives. Whole number data is given the declaration of int, while text uses String. Defaults are set with an equal sign, followed by their value.

Now, as it so happens, I decided to use the same descriptors in both the chair and the table to define them. You might also notice that I could have gone into more detail when describing these particular objects. Let's go back to my friend on the phone, who wants to know more about the objects around me in the coffee shop. Let's say he asks, "What are the shapes of the tabletops? Are the chairs pushed in or pulled out?"

I can simply alter my formulas to the following new equations. Here is my formula for a chair:

```
class Chair {
int legs = 4;
int height = 36;
String material = "Wood";
String position = "Pushed in";
}
```

Here is a formula for a table:

```
class Table {
int legs = 1;
int height = 37;
String material = "Metal";
String shape = "Rectangular";
}
```

Notice that I put a `position` variable on my chair, as the chair can be "pushed in" or "pulled out." The table is stable, and doesn't need this variable. Let's just say that all the chairs are one shape, and I don't need a shape for them. This is not the state of all the tables in our coffee shop, which is why I chose Rectangular for this.

You can imagine what my friend on the phone would think if I altered the information in the variables. If I wanted to heighten my table by 3 inches, I could set its `int height` to 40. I could make my chair look like an octopus if I set `int legs = 8`. I could even have fun and make my table and chair made of marshmallows with `String material = "Marshmallow."`

Yes, I am being quite a code magician. Of course, objects are really boring if just left to themselves. An object's fields, or variables, hold its state. However, it needs some actions associated with it, which is why we use *methods*: programming routines that operate on the object's internal states. These methods are the verbs to the objects' nouns.

Methods

Everything that we have created about our table and chairs are simply default labels. A method will define how these objects act on the variables to define their current operational state. In the case of the chairs, I want them to move back and forth, so people can sit on them.

It's time to create a method, using the void keyword. The method void means that it doesn't return anything, but if you want it to return something, such as an object, you put that afterward.

```
void moveChair (String newPosition) {
```

You will note the method name with lowercase letters followed by uppercase. This is known as *camel case*, and it is a normal method-naming convention that begins with a lowercase letter and then goes to uppercase letters to begin words embedded in the method name, like this: thisIsCamelCase. Also note the first (opening) curly bracket ({). We have to follow that up by a closing curly bracket (}), and something in between the two. So let's add this:

```
void moveChair (String newPosition) {
position = newPosition;
}
```

This basically tells us that we are setting the table's position to that which was passed into the moveChair method.

Let's say I call this in the program, in order to move the chair back. It is as simple as this:

```
moveChair(back);
```

Now, our objects are defined within the class, but they cannot do anything until the user creates an instance of the objects, or *instantiates* them. Let's say I want to define the two chairs at my table; I could use this formula here:

```
Public void onCreate (Bundle savedInstanceState) {
        Super.onCreate(savedInstanceState);
```

```
        setContentView(R.layout.main);

Chair chairOne = new Chair();
        Chair chairTwo = new Chair();

chairOne.moveChair(forward);

        chairTwo.moveChair(back);
```

Were this formula put into a program, we would start with two standard chairs. The new keyword creates that object. We have defined the object Chair, given names to our objects, and set default variable values.

We can use the method thanks to the following code construct:

```
objectName.methodName(variable);
```

In the case of our chairs, I have moved one forward, and one back.

Inheritance

Now let us talk about the concept of *inheritance*. Java supports the development of different types of objects that are more specific in their construction. These more specific objects would be subclassed from the main object. A class that is used for inheritance by a subclass is known as a *superclass*.

For example, I could create a superclass of objects for our chairs and tables known as Furniture. Each of these chairs and tables would be subclasses, and will inherit whatever the superclass has—for example, number of legs, material, height—but I could add specific things for each individual subclass. For example, the position for the chairs and the shape for the tables.

You can create a subclass from a superclass by using the keyword extends, like so:

```
Class Chair extends Furniture {insert new fields and methods here}
```

Interfaces

Certain classes conform to a certain pattern in many Java applications, because the rest of the application should know what to expect of those classes when they are instantiated as objects.

A public interface that the classes present to the application makes their use more predictable and allows the user to use them in places where any class of that pattern is suitable. In the words of programmer Wallace Jackson, who I previously mentioned, "The public interface is a label that tells the application what this class can do, without the application needing to test its capabilities." Implementing an interface is as easy as using an implements command.

The Package Declaration

Recall when I discussed creating an Android application the concept of a *package name*. I am going to go into detail about what it is. This is the first line of code in any Android and Java application. This is written with a keyword and declaration method like this:

```
package application.activity
```

The package concept is like the folder hierarchy that you use on your own computer, and it organizes its code by functionality. The way Android does it is that it organizes its classes into logical packages, which get imported throughout the program.

Programs need `import` statements, which use code from elsewhere. The way I understand `import` statements is like this: if you are writing a book, you will probably need other books as resources to help you. If we look at your Android program as the book you are writing, then the `import` statements are the other books that you need to make your book complete. Android doesn't need a whole library, just a few necessary volumes to do certain things.

In the example that we used with the two chairs, we used the code of `Public void onCreate (Bundle savedInstanceState)`.

This cannot be used unless we import Bundle. This is done as follows:

```
import android.os.Bundle;
```

An `import` statement is usually written in the following format:

```
import platform.functionality.classname;
```

In the case of `import.android.os.Bundle`, it's using the Android platform, with functionality of the os with `Bundle`, allowing the program to create bundles of variables for convenience and organization.

You can find a whole list of packages on the Android Developers web site at `http://developer.android.com/reference/packages.html`. Just so you know, the package isn't the highest level of organization as far as Java is concerned. There is a platform or application programming interface (API). This is a collection of all the core packages for a given language or the packages of a specialized product, like Android.

Getting Your Program to Do What You Want

One of the keys to programming any application in Android is simply figuring out what it is that you want to do, and how to tell Android to do it with code. Fortunately, there have been many who have gone before you, and sometimes it is all about using the same programming code that others have used.

There are places where you can go online to receive help, as there is a community of Android developers who are happy to share their knowledge with you.

The Android Developers Web Site

Believe it or not, the Android development team actually wants you to know how to program on it. It lays out a lot of things that you need to do in order to program on it. The home page can be seen in Figure 12-10; you will remember being on the SDK tab when you had to download the Android SDK.

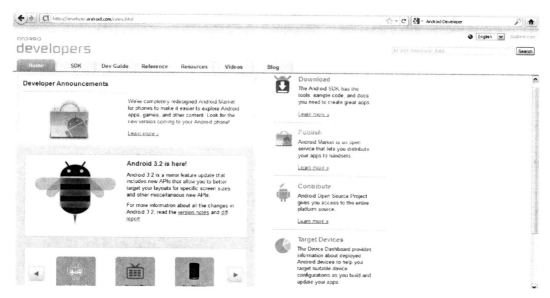

Figure 12-10. The Android Developers site home screen, at http://developer.android.com

The third tab is Dev Guide, and it will help you to understand some of the basics of Android programming. The References tab is also handy because it has a package index and a class index, and the Resources tab is good for articles, tutorials, sample code, and more. The Video and Blog tabs keep a developer in the know as far as new things on Android.

Most of the Android Developers site will seem very confusing at first, but I guarantee that certain things will become clearer when you use it. Note its handy search engine; you can use it to figure out how to make your program do what you want it to do.

Stack Overflow

As you get more adept at programming in Android, you will run into more complex problems with your application. You are going to need answers.

Stack Overflow was created by Jeff Atwood and Joel Spolsky in 2008 for questions and answers about computer programming. You can ask questions and get answers, and usually someone before you has asked the same question. You can see its home page in Figure 12-11, but I guarantee that this has changed by now.

Figure 12-11. The Stack Overflow site, at http://stackoverflow.com/

Other Ways to Find Programming Answers

Of course there are more places to find answers online than just Stack Overflow and the Android Developers site. However, when I have had questions about programming on Android and searched for the answers on Google, these two sites invariably came up in the top ten.

You will find that just doing a search for anything on Google is advantageous. Sometimes you just need to find the right combination of words, such as, "How do I link to Facebook on my Android app?"

Handling Errors in Eclipse

As you are programming your application, you will notice the red lines that come up. There will also be red squares to their left, and red marks on the folders in Package Explorer, as in Figure 12-12. These appear because of errors in your code.

Figure 12-12. *What happens when you get an error on Eclipse*

The Eclipse IDE makes it painfully obvious when your program has errors because your program will not run with them. Your only course of action is to correct them.

Notice that my error in Figure 12-12 is simple spelling. If only all errors were this simple to fix! If you hover your cursor over these errors in the code, Eclipse will tell you what it believes the problem is. It will even tell you how it believes that you can solve the problem. Oftentimes, the error occurs because an import statement is needed, and that is easy to detect when you click the error. Eclipse's suggestions are often quite helpful.

Errors that occur when your program calls upon something that isn't there, however, don't correct themselves automatically. For example, if you set a background, but forget to upload your background to the drawable file, there will be an error. You might find that when you upload the file, you still have the error. You should probably click Refresh or Save All in cases like this. You'll find that the red *X*s should be gone if you have done it right.

Running Applications on Eclipse

Eventually, you have to test your program out in the real world. I highly suggest you do it on an Android device, but you can use the emulator on Eclipse itself.

Creating an Emulator

Here is how you set an emulator up within the Eclipse workspace:

1. Start up Eclipse, and open it to your workspace.

2. Go to the top menu, click Window, and then Android SDK and AVD Manager. You should see a window like you see in Figure 12-13.

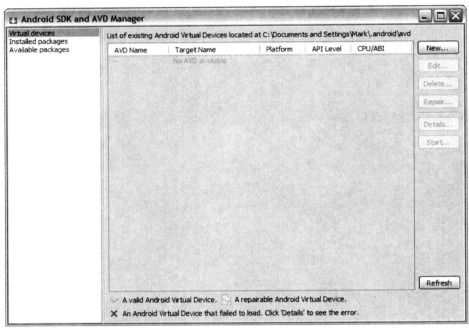

Figure 12-13. Android SDK and AVD Manager, where you can set up an emulator

3. If it is not already selected, click the Virtual Devices column on the left.

4. On the menu on the right, select New. You should see a window like in Figure 12-14.

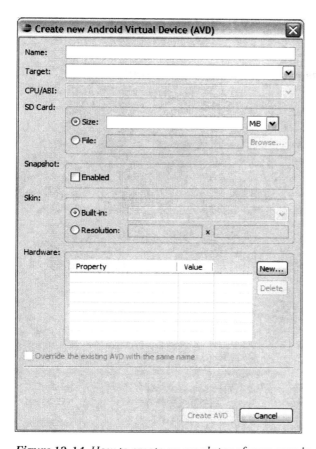

Figure 12-14. How to create an emulator of your own in Android

5. Now it is time to fill in the appropriate information for the Android Virtual Device (AVD). For Name, you can pick anything you want as long as you remember it is an Android emulator. It doesn't accept spaces, so keep that in mind.

6. For Target, select the version of Android that you are working with. The SD Card section can be left blank, you don't need to enable Snapshot, you can leave the skin at its default (HVGA), and you don't need to select anything in the Hardware section.

7. Click Create AVD, and you'll have your emulator. You should see a window like in Figure 12-15.

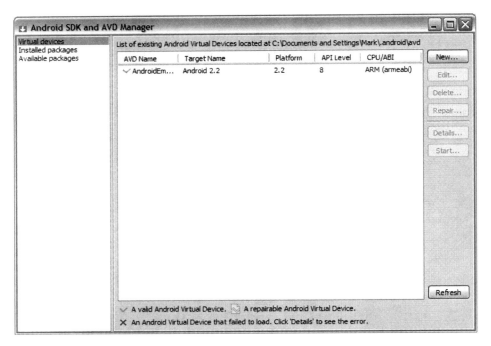

Figure 12-15. Your Android emulator is ready to go!

Running Your Application on Your Emulator

Once you have your program ready and it is error free, your program can be run in several ways:

- You can right-click the top folder in Package Explorer, and select Run As ➤ Android Application.

- Select the application in Package Explorer and click Run on the top menu.

- Select the green arrow at the top and select Run As.

- Select your application and click Ctrl+F11.

If you have chosen to use the emulator on Eclipse, prepare for a long wait. The screen on the left will show all manner of Android logos before it looks like Figure 12-16.. You might have to unlock the emulator like an Android phone, but use your cursor and mouse instead of a finger and touchscreen. That will make sense once it is up and running. You should see your application and interact with it like you would a web site on your computer.

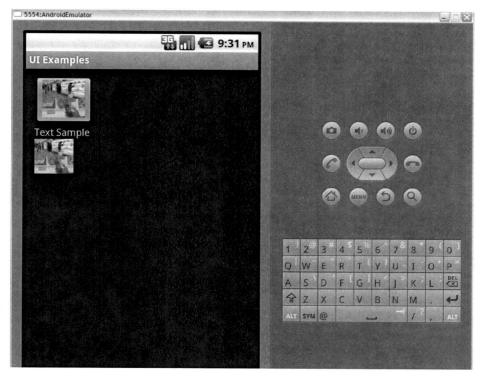

Figure 12-16. *The Android emulator without a device*

I have a five-year-old laptop that I use to write Android programs, and I find that the Eclipse emulator won't do much before it crashes. For this reason and more, I highly recommend using your own Android device. Your application will show up on your Android phone or tablet almost instantly. In fact, the icon for your application will even show up on your home screen menu. The best part is you can use your Android application after you have disconnected your Android device. You will have to have your computer set up to recognize your Android device (I discuss this in Chapter 9 in the "How to Obtain a Screenshot of Your Android Device" section).

Example of an Android Application

The Android Developers web site has a tutorial known as "Hello, World," which allows you to create a simple app that displays text that says anything you want it to say (the tutorial uses "Hello, World," hence its name). You can find this tutorial at http://developer.android.com/resources/tutorials/hello-world.html, but I thought I would set up a program to do something a little more complex in order to demonstrate some of the concepts mentioned earlier.

This program, which I just call New Project, creates two buttons in the center of the screen. One button, labeled "Welcome," creates a dialog that appears in the form of a small, pop-up window. The other button, marked "Website," opens the application to a web site of your own picking.

Go ahead and set up a new program, as shown previously in Figure 12-3. Feel free to use the same names if you like. Once the default folders in Package Explorer appear, open up the main.xml file in the res/layout folder (I explained three ways of doing this earlier). You will see some automated code in the editor. You won't be needing the TextView section, so feel free to highlight and delete the lines of code starting with <TextView to anything before </LinearLayout>. What you should have leftover is this:

```
<?xml version="1.0" encoding="utf-8"?>
<LinearLayout xmlns:android="http://schemas.android.com/apk/res/android"
    android:orientation="vertical"
    android:layout_width="fill_parent"
    android:layout_height="fill_parent"
    >
</LinearLayout>
```

The first line is the default XML declaration, which is made to let Eclipse and Android know precisely what type of file you're using. The next four lines determine the linear layout, which is designed to contain and arrange UI elements placed inside it on the screen horizontally or vertically.

The next three lines configure the settings of the view so Android knows how to view the screen. Note the invoking of android at the beginning of each of them. The line android:orientation="vertical" lets Android know that the view is to be in portrait (not landscape) format. The line android:layout_width="fill_parent" lets the view fill up horizontal space until it reaches its "parent." As for android:layout_height="fill_parent", this is designed to make the layout as tall as possible for the parent.

You may notice in the editor window two tabs in the lower-left corner. One is marked "Graphical Layout" and another "main.xml." Go ahead and select the Graphical Layout option, and you will see exactly what the main screen of your Android application looks like. It is blank for now, but we can fix that. Just add a simple line of code in the LinearLayout section right before the last bracket, like this:

```
<?xml version="1.0" encoding="utf-8"?>
<LinearLayout xmlns:android="http://schemas.android.com/apk/res/android"
    android:orientation="vertical"
    android:layout_width="fill_parent"
    android:layout_height="fill_parent"
    android:background="@drawable/background"
    >
```

I used a picture that I took in Seattle, but you can use anything you want. Just make certain that it is uploaded and sized correctly, as I described previously in the section about how to upload an icon and background. The graphical layout should look something like Figure 12-17.

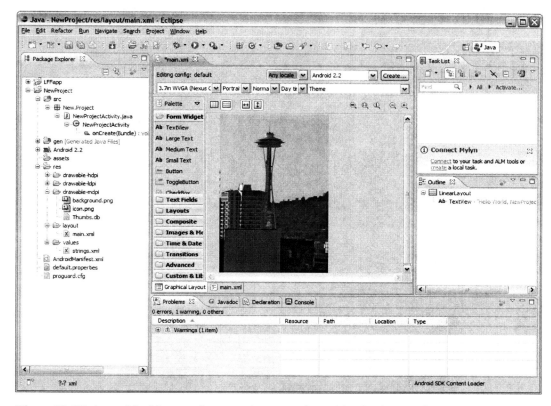

Figure 12-17. *A graphical layout of your project, complete with a background*

In Figure 12-17, you can see an area marked Palette, which is full of file folders. If you click one of these, you can drag and drop some interesting things on your application. For this exercise, go ahead and drag and drop two buttons on your screen, as shown in Figure 12-18.

Figure 12-18. Two buttons have now been added to your Android application.

Notice from Figure 12-18 that you can only put the buttons in two positions, which certainly is boring. LinearLayout is really only designed for simple horizontal or vertical orientation. If you want to change that into something a little more customized, go ahead and click the main.xml tab at the bottom-left corner of the editor and alter the code from LinearLayout to RelativeLayout.

RelativeLayout is a subclass of the ViewGroup class, which allows the user to define how the UI elements are to be placed on the screen relative to each other. There are other subclasses of the ViewGroup as well, including AbsoluteLayout, FrameLayout, and SlidingDrawer, but I won't go into them at this time. You can have the fun of researching and trying them out for yourself.

Go back to the Graphical Layout tab, and you can drag and drop your two buttons into place. Put your buttons in the center of the screen, like in Figure 12-19.

Figure 12-19. *After switching to RelativeLayout and moving your buttons, your application might look like this.*

Notice that if you shift back to the main.xml text, the two Button objects will be automatically coded for you.

From there, you can play with the size of the buttons by going to the Outline section of Eclipse (on the right). By right-clicking the two buttons, you can manipulate their definitions, including their place on the page, what their text reads, and much more. You might want to take some time to play with the characteristics here, just so you can learn how much control you have as a programmer.

You can also just type over the code in the editor itself. For example, you can simply change the text in quotation marks on two of the android:text lines from Button to Welcome and Website, respectively.

Also, it is good to get into the habit of identifying your buttons with something more than just "Button 1" and "Button 2," as this can lead to confusion about what button does what. It is better to name them by their functionality. Notice that I changed the sections marked android:id= to "@+id/btnWelcome" and "@+id/btnWebsite", respectively.

Your code for main.xml for NewActivity should look like the following. Don't worry if it doesn't look precisely like this, as it will depend on where you decide your two buttons will appear on your application.

```
<?xml version="1.0" encoding="utf-8"?>
<RelativeLayout xmlns:android="http://schemas.android.com/apk/res/android"
    android:orientation="vertical"
    android:layout_width="fill_parent"
    android:layout_height="fill_parent"
    android:background="@drawable/background"
    >
<Button android:layout_height="wrap_content"
                android:id="@+id/btnWelcome"
                android:layout_width="wrap_content"
                android:text="Welcome"
                android:layout_alignParentTop="true"
                android:layout_centerHorizontal="true"
                android:layout_marginTop="187dp">
    </Button>
    <Button android:layout_height="wrap_content"
                android:id="@+id/btnWebsite"
                android:layout_width="wrap_content"
                android:text="Website"
                android:layout_below="@+id/btnWelcome"
                android:layout_centerHorizontal="true">
    </Button>
</RelativeLayout>
```

As far as a graphical view, it should resemble Figure 12-20.

Figure 12-20. *What your sample program should look like in graphical layout, provided the main.xml file is programmed with the above code*

Now that we got our main.xml file taken care of, go ahead click src/NewProject/NewProjectActivity and open the NewActivity.java. You will see some already programmed code like this:

```
package New.Project;

import android.app.Activity;
import android.os.Bundle;

public class NewProjectActivity extends Activity {
    /** Called when the activity is first created. */
    @Override
    public void onCreate(Bundle savedInstanceState) {
        super.onCreate(savedInstanceState);
        setContentView(R.layout.main);
    }
}
```

As you can see, the program is already using the concepts of `packages` and `import` statements that I discussed previously. It is also using the principles of inheritance, as `NewProjectActivity` extends `Activity`. You will recognize `public void onCreate` from earlier as well. Those three lines of code after the `@Override` line set your content view to the `main.xml` screen layout XML definition.

Note the comments in between the `/**` and `*/`. Anything entered in between those two symbols will not be read by Android. This is a useful way of describing to others what a certain line or lines of code can do. Comments also come in handy for times when you need to troubleshoot problems with your code. Putting these symbols around areas of code can help you isolate where the problem is.

Let's get back to our program. If you were to run this application now, you would see what's shown in the graphical layout in Figure 12-20. The buttons here are just objects that do nothing when clicked. You could put stickers on your Android device's touchscreen and get the same effect as what you have just programmed. We need to give them methods so they can do their thing.

So how do we make these buttons work? Fortunately, help is easy to find. When I was in this situation, I simply ran a Google search on "Creating a Button on Android." The first result was the Android Developers web site, at `http://developer.android.com/reference/android/widget/Button.html`. You can check it out in Figure 12-21.

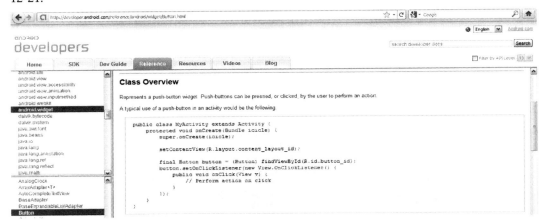

Figure 12-21. *The Android Developers site entry on how to create a push-button widget; one of many entries that can help your application*

In all honesty, I wasn't really certain what this code did when I read the entry in Figure 12-21. But I found that with a little tweaking, I was able to come up with some code that allows a button to perform an action on a click. You will find that the Android Developers site and other similar programmer sites can only give us the materials we need to make our programs work, but the assembly of them is up to you. Here is how I altered the instructions:

```
public class NewProjectActivity extends Activity implements OnClickListener{
```

`OnClickListener` is a particular method that will not work unless we use an import statement. So we need to use it in the above section like so:

```
import android.view.View;
import android.view.View.OnClickListener;
```

Now it is time to really bring these buttons to life. We need to tweak the code yet again to adjust for two buttons:

```
Button btnWelcome = (Button)findViewById(R.id.btnWelcome);
        btnWelcome.setOnClickListener(this);
Button btnWebsite = (Button)findViewById(R.id.btnWebsite);
        btnWebsite.setOnClickListener(this);
    }
public void onClick(View v) {
        Button button = (Button)v;
        //Intent intent;
```

What we are going to need to do now is invoke a Java construct known as a switch, which is like an if...then statement in Android. The case is what we want to happen when our buttons are clicked. For now, we will deal only with the case for the Welcome button, as we need to handle the Website button differently. The default command that you see is what happens if the Website button is clicked.

```
switch (button.getId()) {

case R.id.btnWelcome:
PopupMessage("Welcome to this Application!",  "If everything goes right, you should see this
window.");
                        break;
default:
                        PopupMessage("Something Clicked!", "This button does not do anything
yet.  Please stay tuned!");
                        break;
        }
    }
```

If you enter in the code above, then you will notice an error at PopupMessage. This is because we haven't created the code for PopupMessage yet. We can do that right after our code above, like this:

```
    public void PopupMessage(CharSequence title, CharSequence message) {
        AlertDialog.Builder builder = new AlertDialog.Builder(this);
        builder.setTitle(title)
                .setMessage(message)
                .setIcon(R.drawable.icon)
                .setNeutralButton("OK", new DialogInterface.OnClickListener() {
                        public void onClick(DialogInterface dialog, int which) {
                                return;
                        }
                });
        builder.show();

    }
}
```

In case you are wondering what PopupMessage will do, it should create a dialog window when you click the button. This window will have a title and a message, which you can input in the parentheses after PopupMessage in two sets of quotes, separated by a comma. The PopupMessage window will also bring up the icon, as well as an OK button so we can head back to the main menu.

Were you to run this program, you would discover that the Welcome button puts out whatever message you want. On the right in Figure 12-22, you can see what happens when you click the Website, at least for now.

Figure 12-22. *The dialog window on the left is displayed when the Welcome button is clicked, and the dialog window on the right is displayed when the Website button is clicked.*

The reason why I set up the program to display "Something Clicked" after the Website button is clicked was because I did not know how to make my Android application display a web site view. For situations like this, it is helpful to have some placeholder code until you can get the entire program working properly. This is another trick to programming on Android.

Again, we can find out how to display a web site view on the Android Developers site. If you run a search on WebView on the web site's search engine, you'll find this URL helpful (see Figure 12-23): http://developer.android.com/reference/android/webkit/WebView.html.

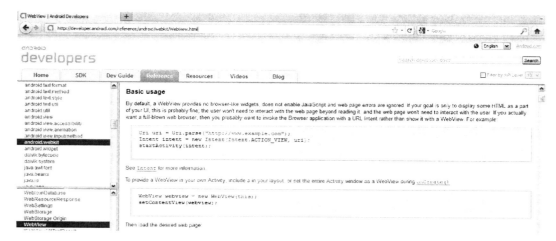

Figure 12-23. *The Android Developers site's instructions for WebView*

We're going to apply the basic usage in Figure 12-23 and make a case for when the Website button is clicked. Go into the NewActivityJava file and add this case to the switch area:

```
case R.id.btnWebsite:
                intent = new Intent(v.getContext(), WebsiteActivity.class);
                startActivity(intent);
                break;
```

The code here states that you are creating a new activity, but you are going to need to do a few things first. Notice that WebsiteActivity is underlined red, because you still need to create this activity. Before that, though, double-check to make certain that you have all your code for NewActivityJava correct.

```
package New.Project;


import android.app.Activity;
import android.app.AlertDialog;
import android.content.DialogInterface;
import android.content.Intent;
import android.os.Bundle;
import android.widget.Button;
import android.view.View;
import android.view.View.OnClickListener;

public class NewProjectActivity extends Activity implements OnClickListener{
    /** Called when the activity is first created. */
    @Override
    public void onCreate(Bundle savedInstanceState) {
        super.onCreate(savedInstanceState);
        setContentView(R.layout.main);
```

```java
        Button btnWelcome = (Button)findViewById(R.id.btnWelcome);
        btnWelcome.setOnClickListener(this);
        Button btnWebsite = (Button)findViewById(R.id.btnWebsite);
        btnWebsite.setOnClickListener(this);
    }
    public void onClick(View v) {
        Button button = (Button)v;
        Intent intent;

        switch (button.getId()) {
            case R.id.btnWelcome:
                    PopupMessage("Welcome to this application!", "If everything goes all
right, you should see this window.");
                    break;
            case R.id.btnWebsite:
                intent = new Intent(v.getContext(), WebsiteActivity.class);
                startActivity(intent);
                break;

                default:
                        PopupMessage("Something Clicked!", "This button does not do
anything yet.  Please stay tuned!");
                        break;
        }
    }

    public void PopupMessage(CharSequence title, CharSequence message) {
        AlertDialog.Builder builder = new AlertDialog.Builder(this);
        builder.setTitle(title)
                .setMessage(message)
                .setIcon(R.drawable.icon)
                .setNeutralButton("OK", new DialogInterface.OnClickListener() {
                        public void onClick(DialogInterface dialog, int which) {
                                return;
                        }
                });
        builder.show();

    }
}
```

Now that you have the NewProjectActivity.java file taken care of, you should make certain that this program will give you a good view of a web site. You will have to open up a new screen for it in your layout file. What you need to do is open res/layout, right-click, select New, and then select Other. You will see a window like in Figure 12-24.

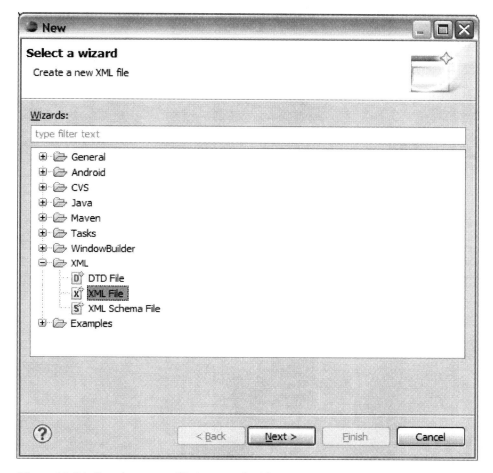

Figure 12-24. Creating a new file in an Android program

Open the XML folder and select XML File. Click Next. You should see a window like in Figure 12-25. Name the file website.xml and click Finish.

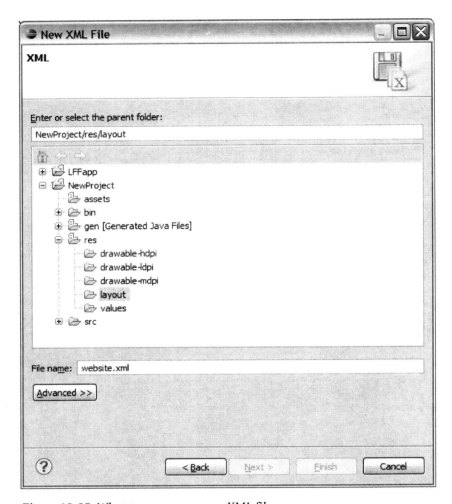

Figure 12-25. What to name your new XML file

Go on and open this file in your editor, and you will see some default code, but not much. Go ahead and add the lines below.:

```
<?xml version="1.0" encoding="utf-8"?>
<WebView xmlns:android="http://schemas.android.com/apk/res/android"
    android:id="@+id/webview"
    android:layout_width="fill_parent"
    android:layout_height="fill_parent"
/>
```

This code tells Android to prepare for a web site view. What web site you want there is up to you. However, you will need to prepare for a new activity in the Java code.

In order to do this, you need to create a new directory by right-clicking the NewActivity.java file. Select New, and then select Class. You'll then see a window like in Figure 12-26.

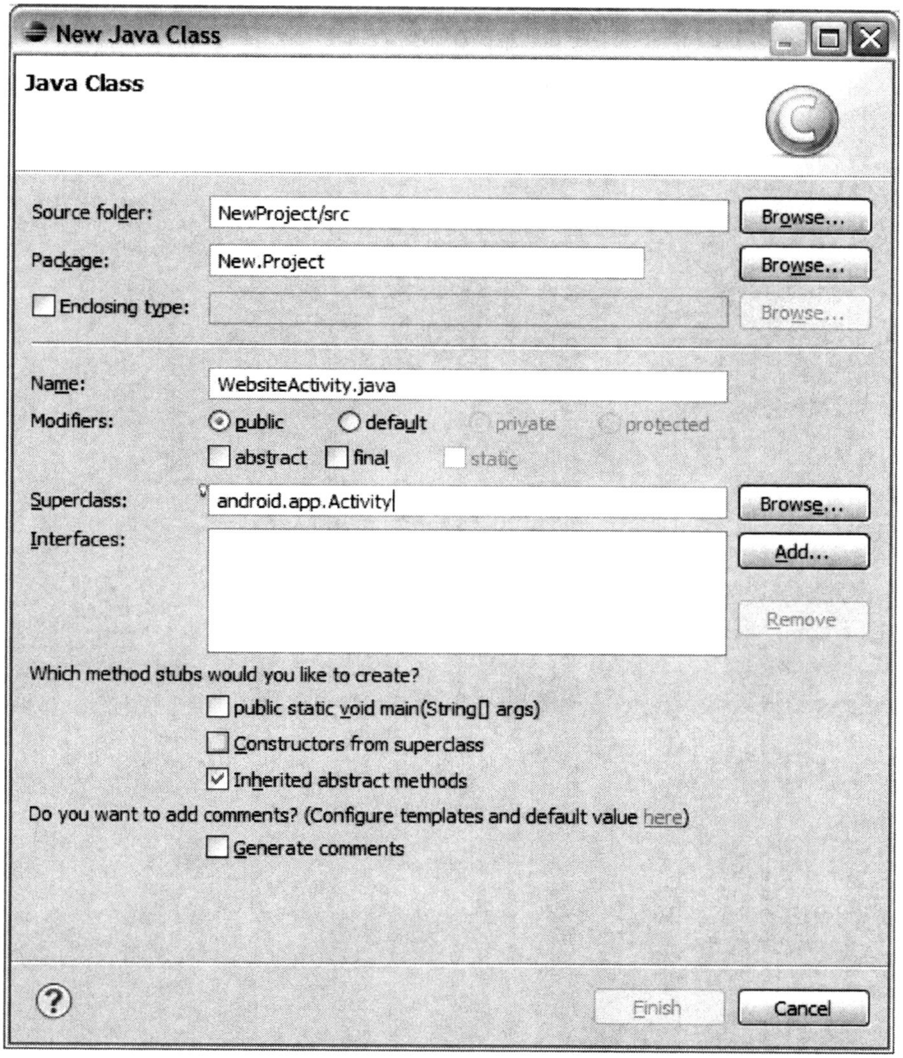

Figure 12-26. Setting up a new Java class in Eclipse

The source folder and package can remain the same. You should choose something like WebsiteActivity.java for the name, and create a superclass of android.app.Activity. Go ahead and click Finish.

Open up `WebsiteActivity.java` in your editor and copy this code:

```java
package New.Project;

import android.app.Activity;
import android.os.Bundle;
import android.view.KeyEvent;
import android.view.View;
import android.view.View.OnClickListener;
import android.webkit.WebView;
import android.webkit.WebViewClient;

public class WebsiteActivity extends Activity implements OnClickListener  {
        WebView webView;

    @Override
    public void onCreate(Bundle savedInstanceState) {
        super.onCreate(savedInstanceState);
        setContentView(R.layout.website);

        webView = (WebView) findViewById(R.id.webview);
        webView.getSettings().setJavaScriptEnabled(true);
        webView.loadUrl("http://google.com");

        webView.setWebViewClient(new HelloWebViewClient());
    }

    public void onClick(View v) {
    }

    private class HelloWebViewClient extends WebViewClient {
        @Override
        public boolean shouldOverrideUrlLoading(WebView view, String url) {
            view.loadUrl(url);
            return true;
        }
    }

    public boolean onKeyDown(int keyCode, KeyEvent event) {
        if ((keyCode == KeyEvent.KEYCODE_BACK) && webView.canGoBack()) {
            webView.goBack();
            return true;
        }
        return super.onKeyDown(keyCode, event);
    }
}
```

Now that we have the XML and Java written, there is one more thing that we need to do. Open up the AndroidManifest.xml program. Right before the last section of

```xml
</application>
</manifest> :
```

put this piece of code to set up the web site:

```
<activity android:name=".WebsiteActivity" android:label="Welcome to the Website"
android:theme="@android:style/Theme.NoTitleBar">
                <intent-filter android:label="Welcome to the Website">
                <category android:name="android.intent.category.DEFAULT" />
          </intent-filter>
      </activity>
```

This lets the manifest know that there will be other activities going on that will cause the changing of screens.

There is one more thing that you need to do before you are ready to publish. You have to ask permission to get on the Internet.

Go ahead and enter in this last line of code at the beginning:

```
<?xml version="1.0" encoding="utf-8"?>
<manifest xmlns:android="http://schemas.android.com/apk/res/android"
    package="New.Project"
    android:versionCode="1"
    android:versionName="1.0">
  <uses-sdk android:minSdkVersion="8" />
  <uses-permission android:name="android.permission.INTERNET"/>
```

Now run the program again. When you click the Website button, it will now direct you to the web site of your choosing (I have chosen Google for this example). You can even click the Back button on your Android device, and you will be directed to the beginning user interface.

If you've made it this far, then you are now an Android developer. You could go to Chapter 9 and publish this on the Android Market if you wished. This is, of course, a very limited program, but in its defense, I have seen Android applications that do less than this. You can see that with a lot of tweaking and more lines of code, the program would be able to do much, much more.

Summary

Programming an Android application with the Eclipse IDE can be difficult, and the user needs to know how Java SE works. Like any OOP language, it uses self-contained constructs known as objects, which are subclassed by a process known as inheritance. The attributes of the objects are determined by the user, and they are put into action by methods, often with the help of package declarations that acquire code from elsewhere.

It really is all about the proper code when writing an application in Eclipse. In fact, it will not work if there are any errors. If you are having trouble figuring out how to program, check out the Android Developers web site, as well as other various online sources; they might have the exact code you are looking for to get your application to do what you want it to do.

You are going to have to use these basic principles to develop an application that is going to make a killing on the Android market. I wish the best of luck to you as you create, innovate, and market your application using the principles in the previous chapters.

Index